THE SCHOOL LIBRARY :
An Educational Tool

THE SCHOOL LIBRARY : An Educational Tool

V. M. Mohanraj
Former Librarian
The Lawrence School, Lovedale
Law College, Chennai
Presidency College, Chennai

Ess Ess Publications
New Delhi

The School Library
An Educational Tool

ISBN : 978-81-7000-635-0

Rs.625/-

First Published 2011

Published by:
Ess Ess Publications
4837/24, Ansari Road,
Darya Ganj,
New Delhi-110 002.
INDIA
Phones: 23260807, 41563444
Fax: 41563334
E-mail: info@essessreference.com
www.essessreference.com

Cover Design by *Patch Creative Unit*

Printed and bound in India at Salasar Imaging Systems.

Contents

Preface

There is a sizable body of literature on school libraries written by school librarians in the United Kingdom and the United States or of any other country. But books on libraries – not on library science but library services – have to be country specific because the social and economic conditions prevailing in each country are different. Books written by school librarians of the UK and the US may not be, therefore, relevant to India *in toto* although some of the ideas could be adapted to suit the conditions prevailing in our country.

Ironically, in India all books on school libraries that I have seen are written by librarians of public libraries, university libraries and library administrators. It should not be misconstrued that I intend to belittle the contributions of librarians of universities and public libraries or library administrators to the corpus of literature on school library. Their contributions, I should say, are invaluable. They can certainly speak on a theoretical plane authoritatively. Hence they deal primarily with technical aspects and look at school library as they do adult libraries, with the result they expect the ethics of libraries for adults to be applied to school library. Above all, it cannot be gainsaid that they do not have any idea of not only the practical problems that a school librarian encounters but also the curricular and co-curricular requirements of school children. In other words, they do not deal with the school library as an extension of class rooms and an instrument of education. We shall discuss these points at the relevant contexts in the chapters that follow.

I am yet to see a book on the school libraries in India written by a school librarian. That is what prompted me to write this book. I had been the librarian of one of the foremost schools in India, the Lawrence School, Lovedale in Tamilnadu for thirty-one years. Prior to that, for eight years, I had worked as college librarian in two of the leading colleges in Chennai – Presidency College and Law College. So I am aware of the needs of school children and school library vis-à-vis the curricular and co-curricular activities of a school and the role of school libraries as a bridge to college/university. I had already written a book, *School Library*, in Malayalam, keeping in view the conditions in Kerala, which was naturally State specific. In that, I have comprehensively dealt with both educational and technical aspects of school library. It was published in 1997 by the Kerala State Institute of Languages, Thiruvananthapuram. The book was well-received by the fraternity of librarians in Kerala. And in my book, *Library Services for Children*, published by Ess Ess Publications, New Delhi in 2004, I have devoted one full chapter to the discussion on library services for school children in particular. I must apologise if the readers find some of the ideas that I have expressed in my book *Library Services for Children* repeated in this. I hope the readers will understand that this is inevitable because the school library is basically one type of juvenile library which caters to one particular class of children, namely school children, and any discussion on library services for children cannot but deal with school libraries.

The Lawrence School in which I worked was a residential co-educational school and had classes from one to twelve. A non-denominational school run on the lines of British Public Schools like Eton and Harrow, it had children and staff from all over India. The school had a very strong and well-equipped library with nearly 50,000 volumes on its shelves and the annual budget was Rs. 1, 50,000 when I superannuated. When I handed over charge in 1989, computer was slowly finding its way into libraries in India and it is heartening to note that the present incumbent, Mondi Murugan, has computerised the catalogue and the circulation section of the library. And the school library is now poised to match the standard of school libraries of developed countries.

A large number of schools in our country still lack proper libraries and many of those that have libraries do not have professional librarians to manage them. S. R. Ranganathan, in his book *Library Development Plan*, published in 1950 had made some suggestions for developing school libraries. And in 1953, the government of India constituted the Secondary Education Commission under the Chairmanship of A. Lakshmanaswami Mudaliar, an educationalist and the then Vice-Chancellor of the Madras university, which in its report, made detailed recommendations* to improve libraries and library services in schools.

At last, in 1962, the Directorate of Extension Programmes for Secondary Education under the Union Ministry of Education did make an attempt to improve library service in schools but State governments as well as the Central government itself did not pick up the thread as

---

* An abstract of the relevant portion of the Report is given in Appendix 1 of my book, *Library Services for Children*, Ess Ess Publications, New Delhi.

expected from where it was left. We shall discus that in detail in chapter 6, 'Resource Persons.' Subsequently, in 1966, another Commission set up under the Chairmanship of D. S. Kothari to suggest measures to revamp school education also recommended certain steps to improve library services in schools. The recommendations that the Commission had made for improving library services in schools, though modest, were also not implemented by the government. In short, the government of India as well as the various State governments had ignored the recommendations of these Commissions with regard to libraries in schools and the Reports of the Commissions were simply allowed to gather dust.

Today the library and the librarian are, as it is said jocularly, in the process of changing to 'cyberary' and 'cyberarian.' The younger generation that is growing up with desktop computers and laptops may in due course prefer digitised documents, popularly known as e-books, to printed ones. As a result the very concept of library is changing. This, perhaps, is a transitional period and it is difficult to forecast what form library as an institution would take in the future.

Interestingly, some of the super book stores have assumed the function of libraries as reading centres. Their objective, of course, is to boost their sales and not that of a library. In order to attract customers they even provide all facilities for those who visit the stores to sit and read and even have vending machines for soft drinks, and beverages on the premises. In fact, public libraries in the US for example, taking the cue from book stores, have now installed vending machines for soft drinks and beverages on their precincts. I think public libraries in our country too should provide such facilities.

Traditionally, a library is a collection of printed materials like books and periodicals, housed in a room or a complex of rooms but the advent of computers and e-books has resulted in the disappearance of the walls of the library.

The computerisation and networking of libraries making centralised cataloguing a possibility in the wake of transformation of printed books into e-books may make the work of classification and cataloguing in school libraries redundant. The reader does not have to know the call number nor does he need a manual catalogue to get a book. He types the title of the book or the name of the author or even a key word in the title and click the "Enter" button on the computer, the book appears on the monitor in front of him. The day when e-library and e-books become a reality is not far off. So I have been thinking of skipping writing on classification and cataloguing but I changed my mind on the advice of Mondi Murugan, the present librarian of The Lawrence School, Lovedale. And I have dealt with these briefly in chapter 7, 'Technical Matters.'

This book must be read in conjunction with two of my other books on the library. The first one, *Library Services for Children*, especially chapters 3, 5, 6 and 7 of which chapter 3 deals with the functions of school library and the others discuss children vis-à-vis different aspects of reading in general. In the second one, *The Multifaceted Librarian*, chapters 6, 7 and 8 deal with technical matters. Of these, although in chapter 6, I discuss principles of book selection in libraries generally, they are applicable to school libraries also. The other two chapters deal with classification and cataloguing. Both these books are published by Ess Ess Publications, New Delhi. So I have refrained from going deep into these topics and only touched upon them in this book.

I have briefly dealt with in Chapter 9, 'Children's Literature,' juvenile literature in English only because it is the one language that is taught in all the states, even if the medium of instruction happens to be any one of the Indian languages. Incidentally, I dealt with children's literature in Sanskrit also because, the Central and Sainik schools as well as Navodaya Vidyalayas and several CBSE schools, apart from many government schools in various states teach Sanskrit as third language. However, the possibility of a student who opts for Sanskrit as third language, taking a book in Sanskrit for general reading is very remote.

Yet I dealt with Sanskrit juvenile literature to bring home to the readers that children's literature had been known to us in those times but was ignored with the rise of local languages for various reasons, a discussion of which is beyond the scope of this book. The living Indian languages are taught mostly in the states concerned only and I must confess except for the history of juvenile literature in Malayalam, I am ignorant of that of other Indian languages. In my book on school library in Malayalam, I have dealt with the history of children's literature in that language.

In Appendix 1, 'Word Games' I have given suggestions to school librarians and primary school teachers for introducing children to alphabetical order through games. I have given only a few of them to show how to teach children what alphabetical order is and the various problems that they may encounter when arranging in alphabetical order. The librarian or/and language teacher should give more complicated ones to make the children fully conversant with alphabetical order before they move on to upper primary classes so that they would have no difficulty in using the library catalogue.

Introduction

There is an unmistakable relationship between the manuscripts or books produced in a given period and the cultural level of the society of that period. The discovery of printing and subsequent improvements in the technique of printing have resulted in mass production of books and periodicals and now the number of books and periodicals coming out of the press all over the world everyday is in thousands. This is not an exaggeration; if anything it is an understatement. As the corpus of books produced burgeons, an institution is called for to store those books and make it available to the contemporary and future generations. That institution is the library. It may not be wrong to say, therefore, that the strength of the library movement is an indication of the cultural and the educational standard of a people. At the same time the higher the level of educational and cultural standard of the people, the greater the demand for books and libraries. There is, thus, a dialectical relation between the production of books and the educational and cultural level of the people.

As far as we know today, the institution known as library made its appearance in the world in the 3rd millennium BCE in the Babylonian town of Nippur. The first librarian that we know of was Herodotus of Ephesus, a Homerian scholar, who was in charge of the famous Alexandrian library founded by Ptolemy I or Ptolemy II in the 3rd century BCE. The digital revolution is posing a challenge to traditional notion of the institution of library. Electronic books, popularly known as e-books are slowly but steadily replacing printed books and possibly in the not too distant future, libraries of printed books with which we are familiar today will have to yield place to digital libraries!

There is a mistaken notion obviously created by the British colonialists and their apologists that library is an institution which India inherited from the West. Those who hold this view are totally ignorant of our indisputable library heritage and those who refuse to accept the contribution of the West to our library movement are blind to reality. Our civilisation goes back to thousands of years and the library movement in India has a very long history. But when we look back through the thick wall of Time, we will not be able to see the various types of libraries that constitute our library movement today. The school library, for example, is a recent addition to our library movement. There is no gainsaying the fact that it is the foundation on which stands the modern library movement in the country. The reason is obvious. It is there, in the school library, that library consciousness is instilled in children, who constitute the prospective clientele of the various types of libraries.

However, the root of library movement in India runs deep into the past. It is surmised there were libraries in our country thousands of years back, in *circa* 2600 BCE, when the pre-Harappan civilisation thrived in the Indus Valley. Although discovery of alphabet may be traced back to the period of the Indus Valley civilisation, the materials used for writing were stone and pointed chisel. Archaeologists have exhumed many such stones with inscriptions at Harappa and Mohenjo Daro and these documents on stones do not call for a library.

However, two items, one each from Mohenjo Daro and Chahnu Daro, resembling inkpots had been unearthed and the stone inscriptions prove beyond doubt that the people of the Indus Valley had a script too. Some historians think that in those times writing was done on barks, leaves or some other similar material. Archaeologists had also exhumed clay seals and tablets bearing pictographs from various sites in the Valley. All these suggest that writing was known to the civilised people of the Indus Valley at that time. Possibly, therefore, there were written documents, which would have accumulated, pointing to the possibility of libraries being there. But no building that could be construed as a library has so far been unearthed at any of those sites. So as far as we know today, there were no libraries in the Indus Valley. The written records, if there had been any, must have been destroyed at the time of Aryan influx or even earlier in the floods that had inundated the region on several occasions as well as in the tectonic disturbances that destroyed Mohenjo Daro. Perhaps, we shall have to revise these conclusions when those inscriptions on stones are deciphered

Interestingly, the barbaric pastoral Aryan tribes that had been migrating to India intermittently during that period had settled in the region. They did not know writing and their literature consisting of the Vedas and the Vedangas were taught and transmitted from generation to generation orally. The exact date when the Vedic corpus was reduced to writing has not been determined although there is abundant evidence to believe that this could have been at the turn of the tenth century BCE, almost coinciding with the Mahabharata War.

Macdonnel, the well-known Indologist points out, Professor Buhler's palaeographical researches had revealed that the ancient Indians used two types of scripts – Kharoshti and Brahmi. The former had been used since the 4th century BCE till about the 2nd century CE and was confined to the Gandhara kingdom, which encompassed Eastern Afghanistan and the Northern Punjab of today. This script was of the Aramaic type of the Semitic writing and was written from left to right. The Brahmi script, he says, was based on the oldest Northern Semitic or Phoenician writing and was probably brought to India in *circa* 800 BCE by traders coming via Mesopotamia. This script was employed in the rest of India and he opines that the later Indian alphabets were derived from it.

The testimony of Quintus Curtius Rufus, the Roman historian known for his work on Alexander the Great, Macdonnel states, shows that birch leaf (*bhujra patra*) was being used in north India for writing on in as early as the 4th century BCE, that is at the time of Alexander the Great (356-323 BCE). The birch leaf had been in use in north India because the birch (*Betula jacquemontii*) grows only in the sub-tropical climate of the Himalayan region. In the peninsular India they were using palmyra leaf (*thaali patra*) instead of birch leaf and metal stylus was used to write on it. This is the leaf of palmyra palm (*Borasses flabillifer*).

It can be said with certainty that writing and production of literature were prevalent in the period of Panini, who is generally believed to have flourished in the 4th or 5th century BCE. As Macdonell states, "the actual use of ink is proved for the second century BCE by an inscription from a Buddhist relic mound and is rendered very probable for the fourth century BCE." However, nothing that was written in those days were collected and preserved. Whatever manuscripts of those times are extant today had been in the palaces of kings or in some of the houses of the high caste Hindus and so 'library' as an institution was unknown to the Indo-Aryans.*

The seed of the library movement in India may be said to have been sown by the Buddhist monasteries, of which we come to know from the travelogues of Chinese pilgrims, like Fa-Hsien, Hieun-Tsang and I-Tsing. Fa-Hsien visited India in the fifth century CE, followed by Hieun-Tsang and I-Tsing in the seventh century. They have given eye-witness accounts of the Buddhist monastic libraries they visited, which speak volumes for the library movement and library services in our country in those days. Apart from these Chinese travellers, Buddhists pilgrims from other countries of the Far East like Japan and Korea also had visited this country to study Buddhism and transcribe Buddhist texts, which were in the monastic libraries. It may, therefore, be presumed that the history of the library movement in India commences several years before the 5th century CE, probably during the life time of the Buddha himself.

All important Mahayana viharas had their own libraries and many libraries in India grew up as adjuncts to Buddha viharas, monasteries, universities and palaces all over India. The library was then known by various terms. Interestingly, saraswathi mahal, saraswathi bhandar, pusthaka bhandar, jnana bhandar, bharati bhandagaras, grantha kuti, kitab khana were some of the terms used for 'library.' Those libraries that grew up long before printing was discovered were rich store houses of many invaluable manuscripts written on palm leaves, birch bark and such other materials.

* Macdonell, A.A., A History of Sanskrit Literature, Motilal Banarsidas, Delhi, 1971, p. 14-16.

In South India, the libraries, known as saraswathi bhandaras or pusthaka bhandaras, were established as inevitable annexes to the pathashalas (schools) attached to temples and monasteries. These were all humungous establishments housing huge collections of manuscripts. That six librarians were appointed to supervise the library established by king Thrailokyamallan (1058 CE) of the Chalukya dynasty in Nagai, indicates how big the library was. The stone inscriptions found in the Perumal temple at Kancheepuram states that a person by name Vasishnadasan had been entrusted to establish a matth and library attached to the temple. Although comparatively small, this library was a very important one that could not be ignored. Another library that was equally important was the one attached to the Sringeri matth. There are extant records stating that the king of Vijayanagar who ruled in 1406 CE had donated four villages to the poet Krishna Bhatta, who was the then librarian, to renovate and run that library.

Although there were many such pusthaka bhandaras in South India, the largest collection of palm leaf manuscripts and books were in the Saraswathi Mahal (also known as Maharaja Serfoji's Saraswathi Mahal Library) at Thanjavur in Tamil Nadu. This was established by the Telugu Naickars who ruled Thanjavur in the 16th century CE and it may not be wrong to say that this is one of the few libraries of the mediaeval period that still exists in the world. Today, this library has 3780 Tamil manuscripts, over 800 Telugu manuscripts, 3076 Marathi manuscripts and 1342 bundles of a total of over 250,000 Raj records written in Modi script of the Marathi language. Apart from these there are over 4500 old books in English, French, German, Italian and Greek. There are also more than 420,000 books in Sanskrit, Marathi, Telugu and Hindi,

Although there were no libraries of all-India fame in the region, which now forms Kerala State there were numerous small libraries all of which contained good collections of valuable palm leaf manuscripts. Called granthappura in Malayalam, these were in the palaces of the Rajas and the houses of chieftains of the various principalities. Many landlords, irrespective of their religion or caste, who were educated, had granthappuras or collections of palm leaf manuscripts in their houses.

India witnessed the sprouting of libraries during the five centuries, from the 9th to the 13th century, when there was an unprecedented spurt in literary activity as a result of what is known as the Bhakthi movement. In the western India, libraries grew up as an inevitable result of the spread of Jainism in the region. The centres in which these libraries sprung up were primarily Jaisalmer, Pattan, Surat, Cambay, Ahmedabad, Dholkar, Karnavathi and Vijapur. The roles played by two kings – Sidharaja Jayasimha (CE 1049-1143) and Sreekumarapaladeva (CE 1143-1174) – in the advancement of the Jain library movement is commendable and cannot be over-emphasised. During their reign, Pattan, the capital of the kingdom, was an important centre of the library movement. After Siddharaja Jayasimha conquered Malwa in CE 1140, he transferred the Imperial library of Bhojaraja in Dhara to Anhilvad and merged it with the library of the Chalukya kings. There are historical documents stating that Srikumarapaladeva established twenty-one jnanabhandaras (libraries) containing large number of manuscripts. And emulating these kings, their ministers also took keen interest in the development of libraries and the library movement. The well-known among them were Amar Bhatta, Vag Bhatta and Srivastupala-tajpala who is known to have established three huge libraries spending crores of 'ponpana' (the then currency). But most of the Jaina jnhanabhandaras established during that period were later gutted by the fire of religious frenzy.

A word about the library of Bhojaraja of the Paramara dynasty. All the Paramara kings who ruled Malwa in the 10th and the 11th centuries were great patrons of learning and literature. They were great book lovers too. Bhojaraja who reigned from CE 1018-1060, was himself a very learned man and writer. His works included poetry, philosophy, yoga, phonetics, medicine, veterinary science and archery. He established a university in Dhara and the famous library of the period was housed in the same building. This library contained the works of the kings of Malwa as well as those of the contemporary scholars and poets.

Two of the important centres of the Western Indian library movement were Vallabhi and Kanheri. The library attached to the mahavihara at Vallabhi which was patronised and lovingly nurtured by the Maithraka kings who ruled from CE 475 to 775 was famous all over India attracting scholars from far and near. The state treasury, it is said, had set apart a huge amount for procuring manuscripts for this library. Another library that was comparable to Vallabhi was the one attached to Kanheri matth. This matth and the library were established with the generous contribution of a Jain devotee, Gomin Avighnakara who hailed from Gauda. He did not forget to set apart a certain amount for purchasing manuscripts for the library. The golden era of this library was from CE 821 to 867, when Amoghavasrsha of the Rashtrakuta dynasty was on the throne. Mahaveera who authored *Ganitasara Samgraha*, Gunabhadra who wrote *Mahapurana* and several such famous scholars like Jinasena, Virasena and

Shakatayan flourished during this period. The works of all these scholars enriched the Kanheri matth library.

The Eastern and Central regions of India too had strong library movements. Some of the famous universities like the Nalanda, Vikaramasila, Somapuri, Jaggadal and Mithila that dotted this region had well-stocked libraries. The most famous of these was the library of the University of Nalanda. Situated approximately sixty-four kilometres to the west of Patna, this was an insignificant village, unheard of in the 5th century. But soon this developed as a world renowned centre of education and along with it, a library known as Dharmaganhjam too grew up. This library consisted of three huge buildings called Rathnasagaram, Rathnodadhi and Rathnaranhjakam and all sacred texts were stacked in Rathnodadhi, a nine-storeyed building. Many of the collections were lost during the Muslim invasion in the 12th century. Although a monk called Mutithabhadra got all these buildings repaired, they did not exist for long after that. The buildings were finally destroyed when two mendicants who were insulted by two inmates of the matth, set fire to them and unfortunately, Rathnodadhi too was consumed by this inferno of flames.

Vikramasila monastery, situated about thirty-nine kilometres to the east of Bhagalpur in Bihar, was established in the 8th century CE by King Dharmapala. The University and the library of this monastery had many manuscripts in Sanskrit and Tibetan languages and for nearly four centuries these reigned supreme as a centre of learning. But this university and the library along with the matth of which those were adjuncts, were razed to the ground when Bhakthiar Khilji invaded this kingdom. Another library that Bhakthiar Khilji destroyed was the one attached to the Odantapuri mahavihara. This library built in CE 749 was a rich depository of innumerable

Buddhist and Brahminical works, during the reign of king Mahipala I.

The library of the Somapuri University, which was a reputed centre of learning since the reign of king Dharmapala (CE 769-827) was destroyed in the 11th century by a fire, the cause of which had not been mentioned in any extant document. Later a monk by name Vipul Mitra renovated it but it did not regain the fame that it had earlier. Three other reputed libraries in Bengal were those of the viharas of Jaggadal, Devikatha and Panditha. All three of these libraries which had a vast collection of Buddhist religious literature were well-known in the 11th and 12th centuries.

Another library that had attained great fame during this period was in Mithila. The students who studied at the university of which this library was an adjunct, were expected to deposit in the library all their notes and copies of manuscripts that they had made during the course of their study. In fact, it was a convention, rather an unwritten law of the university. The value of the notes preserved in the library may be gauged when it is said that Sankara Misra who wrote *Padartha Chandra*, Gangesa Upadhyaya, the founder of Neo-logical school of philosophy, who authored *thathva chinthamani*, and Vachaspathi Misra who wrote commentaries on *Gita Govindam*, *Malathi Madhavam*, *Devi Mahathyam*, *Bhagavadgita*, *Meghadooth* and such other works were a few of those students. This library which had many valuable manuscripts retained its all-India fame till the end of the 15th century.

Apart from all these, the Imperial libraries maintained by the kings of Mysore, Bikaner, Alwar, Jammu-Kashmir and other Rajas and Nawabs cannot be overlooked. That Hieun-Tsang was tempted to spend two years in the Imperial library of the king of Kashmir, points to the extent and value of the collection in that library.

The early Muslim rulers did not have separate buildings for the Imperial libraries. The collection of manuscripts was jealously guarded and kept within the four walls of their palaces and mosques. That it had an inhibitive effect on the library movement cannot be denied. Nevertheless, it did not limit the growth of the library movement and the number of libraries increased considerably during the Muslim period. The Sultanate period (CE 1206-1526) witnessed the proliferation of kitabkhanas (libraries) and they appointed profound scholars only as librarians whose primary function was to supervise and run these libraries, which shows the great importance that the Sultans attached to libraries. The kitabdar or mushafbardar that is, librarian of the library established by Jalaluddin Khilji was Amir Khusrau who was a great Persian scholar and Sufi poet. Some of the other librarians were Moulana Muaiyyan-ud-din Umrani who was one of the most respected scholars of Islamic thought and Minhaj-ud-din and Zia-ud-din Barni who were distinguished historians.

During the period of the Tughlaq dynasty also the library movement was as vibrant as it had been till then. Even a courtier of Firuz Shah, Tatar Khan who was a great scholar and a commentator of Qur'an had his own private library with an invaluable collection of works on Islamic religion. Encouraged and patronised by Sultan Sikandar Lodhi, Kitabkhanas sprung up all over the country during his reign. All the nobles and courtiers had their own private kitabkhanas. Interestingly, after the First Battle of Panipat marking the end of the Delhi Sultanate and the establishment of the Mughal Empire in India, in 1526, the Mongol prince Zahir ud-Din Muhammad, popularly known as Babur, took over the private library of Ghazi Khan, a courtier of Sultan Ibrahim Lodhi, the last king of the Delhi Sultanate.

Babur made it mandatory so to say, to have kitabkhanas or libraries for all *madrassas*, as Islamic educational institutions were (and still are) called. This, in fact, was analogous to the school library of modern times and shows how conscious he was of the importance of libraries in educational institutions. All Mughal emperors, without exception, took a keen interest in organising and establishing libraries in the country. Humayun and Akbar were the two among the Mughal emperors who took the greatest interest in the library movement. Humayun's private library is said to have contained a large number of rare manuscripts. He was so much interested in libraries that he even converted the luxurious house, Sher Mandal, which was constructed by Sher Shah in 1541, in Purana Qila into a library. Besides, he constructed a building complex called Khana-e-Tilism in Agra and the upper storey of a magnificent octagonal building known as Khana-i-Sa'dat, which was at the centre of this complex, was made a library. It is said that Humayun was so fond of books that he even carried a library of selected books with him and took his librarian too during his expeditions. Even when he was in self-exile in Cambay after he was defeated by Sher Shah, he had a collection of books – many of which were rare – and his librarian with him. It is significant that he died of a fatal fall from the stairs of his library.

His son, Akbar, succeeded him to the throne and it is said, he was not a literate. Nevertheless, he loved books as much as or perhaps much more than his father did and took as much interest as his father in promoting library movement. He also patronised writers and artistes and his court was illumined by the famous 'nine gems' that included, to name a few, Tansen the renowned musician, Birbal, known for his wit, Abdul Rahman Khan-I-Khana a great poet in Persian and Sanskrit. His Imperial library, it is not an exaggeration to say, had no parallel either in India or in any other country in the world at that time. He collected books from all quarters, private libraries and libraries of his tributary kingdoms, thus enriching the Imperial library. He brought collections of books from the palaces in Kashmir, Bengal, Gujarat, Deccan to name some, and added them to his collection. After his death when an inventory of his possessions was taken, it was found, there were twenty-four thousand illustrated manuscripts in his library

The Muslim rulers of South India too were as much interested in the library movement as those in the North. For instance, Tipu Sultan had a library of not less than two thousand invaluable books. After his death and with the fall of Seringapatam (Srirangapatnam) in 1799 in the Fourth Mysore War, the victorious British imperialists confiscated his library. But the British officers could not appreciate the value of those books and as a result of their indifference in taking care of the collection, many of the valuable books were damaged. All those damaged books were discarded as garbage and of the remaining ones, a few were sent to London and the rest transferred to the Fort William College in Calcutta (Kolkata) and the Bengal Asiatic Society Library.

Printing press was introduced in India by the Portuguese in 1556, with the establishment of the first press in Goa. As far as it is known, the first book printed in India was St. Xavier's *Doutrina Christa*, in Portuguese language in 1557 and the first book in an Indian language to be printed was the Tamil translation of the same book in 1578. The first library of printed books in our country was inaugurated in 1663-'64 in the Fort St. George in Madras (Chennai), after which many small libraries containing nothing but books on Christianity sprung up in various parts of the country. In the first half of the 18th century, public libraries were started in Calcutta (Kolkata), Madras (Chennai) and Bombay (Mumbai). With the amalgamation of the Calcutta Public Library and the Calcutta Secretariat Library in 1903 the Imperial Library came into existence and after India attained independence this was turned into the National Library.

Belvedere House which now houses the National Library stands on a ground with an area of 120,000 m^2. This was formerly the Viceregal Palace where the Governor-General of India and later the Governor of Bengal resided. The building was constructed some time in the second half of the 18th century. Mir Jafar Ali Khan, the then Nawab of Bengal, who was forced to abdicate and shift to Calcutta where he was put up within the fortifications of the East India Company at Alipore, constructed many buildings on the land he possessed. Belvedere House was one of them and he gifted it to Warren Hastings who was the Governor-General at that time.

The birth of another library can be traced back to the founding of the Literary Society of Bombay in 1804. This society which was started with the objective of promoting the study of Indology was affiliated to the Royal Asiatic Society which was established in 1823 in London. And since 1830 it was called the Bombay Branch of the Royal Asiatic Society. In 1873 the Bombay Geographical Society and in 1896 the Anthropological Society of Bombay merged with it. Seven years after independence, in 1954, its name was changed to the Asiatic Society of Bombay. This name too was naturally changed when the name of Bombay was changed to Mumbai in 2002 and now it is known as the

Asiatic Society of Mumbai. Housed in the colonnaded Town Hall, today this library has a collection of 800,000 rare volumes, one of them being the priceless first edition of Dante's "Inferno" of which there are only two copies in the world including this. This library which was exclusive to the Europeans during the British period is now a public library open to all.

A public library was founded in Madras (Chennai) in 1861 as part of the Museum and it was decided to provide the library with a separate building, for which Lord Connemara, the then Governor of Madras Presidency laid the foundation stone in 1890. This building, which was formally inaugurated on the 5th of December 1896, was named after Lord Connemara. In 1974, it was extended by adding a three-storeyed building with a plinth area of 50,000 sq ft. and in 1999 as a part of centenary celebrations, another three-storeyed building with a floor area of 21,235 sq. ft. was added. The Connemara Library as it is still called, has very rare books, like *Hortus Indicus Malabaricus*, 12 volumes, 1678-1703 and *Flora Indica*, 1768 in its collection. The Delivery of Books and Newspapers (Public Libraries) Act 1954 makes it incumbent on publishers in India to send a copy each of all publications to these three libraries. Hence these libraries – The National Library in Kolkata, The Asiatic Library in Mumbai and the Connemara Library in Chennai – are called National Depository Centres.

There is evidence to say that libraries for the European settlers in Bengal had existed in the 18th century itself but they were all too small to be taken into consideration and perhaps mostly collections of books on Christianity with a few classics of English literature. It is known that the Fort William College in Calcutta (Kolkata) had started a library in 1800. Nevertheless, the preparation of a register of libraries by the government of what was then the Bombay Presidency in1830 is considered the beginning of the modern library movement in India.

The indigenous Library Movement in our country may be said to have been inaugurated with the formation of the Madras Library Association at the All-India Library Conference held in 1927, the initiative for which was taken by none other than the doyen of libraries in India, Dr. S.R.Ranganathan. Although it was called All-India Library Conference, it was then practically confined to the then Madras Presidency comprising the present Tamil Nadu, Kerala, Karnataka and Andhra Pradesh minus what is known as the erstwhile native states. That it was intended to encompass the whole of India is indicated by calling it All-India Library Conference. This organisation concentrated on developing public libraries and expanding their services to the people at large but did not think of the necessity for libraries in schools. Unfortunately, even today, this organisation pays scant attention to school library movement.

Among the native states, Travancore (Thiruvananthapuram) and Baroda (Vadodara) were the only States in which there were library movements worth the name. While in Travancore (Thiruvananthapuram) State it was a people's movement, in Baroda (Vadodara) State it was the result of the initiative taken by the then Gaekwad (king) of Baroda but the latter preceded the former by about a couple of decades. In this connection, it must be put on record that in Kerala State, thanks to the people-based Granthasala Prasthana (The Kerala Library Movement) which has been supported by the government, almost every village has a library today. But those who spearheaded the library movements in either of these states did not think of the necessity for schools to have libraries. They did not realise that the school library is the basis of the library movement, being the producer of the prospective clientele of public and other types of libraries. Of course, the situation in the country was not ripe enough to conceive of libraries in schools. The school library is basically an instrument of education and it did not fall within the purview of the philosophy of education in the India of that period. The then philosophy of education in our country which was then a British colony was defined by Macaulay's 'Minute.' We shall discuss this in Chapter 1, 'School Library — Its Rise and Organisation.

The school library must act as a window that opens on to the rich and ancient heritage of our great country while at the same time relating it to the values of modern India in particular and the world in general. It may sound paradoxical when I say school libraries must do this through open access to all, literate and illiterate, giving them an opportunity to acquire the knowledge required to function as responsible citizens of a democratic society. There is no doubt that with the advent of computers and virtual library and the prospects of the traditional libraries turning into digital libraries, as a result of e-books replacing printed ones, the possibility of public and academic libraries of which the school library is the most important, achieving this objective is enhanced immeasurably.

The digital library has been made possible thanks to the development of e-books and the internet. Its immense reach with the potential for providing not only information but documents as well, from any part of the world in a matter of a few minutes would in the not too distant future practically globalise libraries. It will bring before your eyes the changes that had come about in our society at different points of time and the personalities that helped steer the society in the right or wrong direction at such critical junctures. It will also help present vividly social, cultural, political and other aspects of human society. The seekers of information would not have to go to archaeological sites to see the remains of ancient world or to places concerned to refer to historical documents. The computer terminal will bring them in all their vividness in front of the student researching them or to the cursory reader who is interested in them.

Some librarians fear that the increasing use of computers at home or virtual library that is, a worldwide collection of online printed documents available on the internet is a threat to the existence of the institution of library in general and consequently school libraries too will become redundant. This is a mistaken notion. The sweep of the virtual library is limited because individuals may not be able to access all the documents or resource materials that he needs or is interested in. Many information databases cannot be accessed gratis on the internet, as these have to be subscribed to, which will be beyond the purse of a majority of individuals. And when most books are published in electronic form and e-books become popular many e-books too would demand fees for accessing them. Today, several on-line journals, books and other records restrict access to subscribers only. Those who do not subscribe to those documents individually, access them through libraries of which they are bona fide members or schools/colleges at which they study or business/industrial houses for which they work. This is possible because all of them would be institutional subscribers. A person with an active library membership number will be able to access all kinds of documents by virtue of his membership. The membership fee for a public library is affordable by a vast majority of the people and so libraries cannot be sidelined and will not become irrelevant.

The virtual library will have no adverse effect on it; if anything, it will only enhance its effectiveness. In fact, virtual library will supplement all types of libraries, making it easier for individuals who are, for example, members of a library to retrieve information. As far as the school library is concerned, as we shall discus in detail in chapter 2, 'Aims of the School Library' and chapter 3, 'Methods in the Library' it has definite educational aims and these can be achieved only by the school library working in tandem with the school and virtual library can doubtless supplement the school library. In other words, no school library can function independently of the school and *ipso facto* virtual library cannot replace the school library because it cannot carry out the functions of a school library.

Whatever type of library it is, whether public, academic or special, traditional or digitised, the library is basically a welfare organisation as its services and programmes are educationally oriented and is run in the interest of the society or the community that it serves. Naturally, therefore the onus of establishing and funding this institution is on the government, whether central, state or local. In the case of libraries of government and aided schools, the government or local government as the case may be, gives necessary grants to the schools concerned for maintenance of the school building which includes the library building and for replenishing the equipment and resources of the library. In the case of private schools, it is for the management to provide in the budget necessary funds for the upkeep and development of the library.

Dr. Rangnathan has stated five principles on which

every library functions or ought to function. However, looking at them from a technical perspective, there are some essential pre-requisites for these principles to be put into practice. When he says "books are for use," he recognises the necessity to make it easy for the readers to make use of the books in the library and that implies that library rules should not be inhibitive. In other words, the rules of the library should be so framed as to facilitate not only recreational reading but research as well without any restrictions whatsoever. And that, of course, presupposes open access system. If the other two principles, "Every reader his book" and "Every book its reader," have to be implemented, the books that are purchased have to be arranged in such a way that the reader would be able to lay his hands on the book or books he wants. This points to the need for properly classifying and cataloguing the resources of the library. The fourth law, "Save the time of reader" implies committed library staff as well as a simple charging system. That the library needs to be enriched by regularly adding new books is implicit in the last law, that "The library is a growing organism." All these five principles call for an efficient and committed library staff, without which all these would remain hollow words.

1

School Library — Its Rise and Organisation

The changes in the socio-economic system of society, the discovery of printing press, the introduction of universal education and the consequent cultural progress in general made the educationalists, educators and educational authorities aware of the inadequacy of school libraries. Not just that – the conditions favourable to make it practicable also were present. It was at the end of the second decade of the twentieth century that educationalists, educators and educational authorities accepted that library was an integral part of any school and realised the urgency of providing libraries in schools and setting standards for school libraries.

Few librarians and educationalists are aware that the concept of library as an integral part of the school actually materialised when on May 30, 1918 the Soviet government under the leadership of Lenin passed a decree on libraries. By the next decade this idea began to be accepted by the western countries too. Among the countries of the West, the one in which the school library came into existence first was the US with the publication of standards for library organisation and equipment by the National Education Association in 1920. And eight years later, in 1928, with the submission of Board of Education's 'Memorandum on Libraries in State-aided Secondary Schools,' the school libraries began to appear in the Secondary Grammar Schools in the UK. The Memorandum stated that it was "an indispensable part of every secondary school," and this was tantamount to making it compulsory for every Secondary Grammar School in England to have its own library. This was followed by a report on 'Books in Public Elementary Schools' which stressed the necessity for libraries in secondary modern schools. Three years later, in 1931, a government publication, the 'Suggestions for the Planning of New Buildings for Secondary Schools' made it obligatory for every secondary school in England to have a library. Nevertheless, secondary schools did not have adequate libraries either in the US or in the UK.

When India was under the British rule, schools were intended to produce what they called the 'writers' (clerks) to keep the books of the colonial machinery and not for imparting real education to the children in the country. In Macaulay's words that reflect arrogant chauvinism, the schools were meant "to form a class who may be interpreters between us and the millions whom we govern – a class of persons Indian in blood and colour but English in tastes, in opinions, in morals and in intellect."* The British imperialists were interested in imparting the three R's and minimum necessary knowledge of commercial mathematics, history, geography and science to the children in India. The stress was on commercial mathematics and English language. So no school had what may be termed a library, an institution that had not developed in schools even in their own country.

However, by third decade of the 20th century, educational rules were framed stipulating that every school had a library with a certain minimum number of volumes, for which the government gave an ad hoc grant. The grant given by the government for the purchase of books was a pittance; this was usually a meagre amount hardly sufficient to purchase about nine or ten books at the most. The school authorities bought the few books, abridgements of some classics and a few, if any, children's books that they could get with that allotment and stuffed the so-called library with all sorts of books they could get gratis to make up the mandated number of volumes. So the school libraries of those times were motley collections and not balanced selections of books. These collections of books were there primarily to be shown to the officer of the Education Department who visited the school every year when he would verify if the school had utilised the grant given by the government for the purchase of library books, as required by the rules and if the school had the stipulated number of books in the library. The rules did not specify what type of books the school library should have; nor did they state what had to be done with these books. Hence the educational administrators were also not concerned with those matters.

Unlike as it is today, in those days all textbooks, except the English textbook for Form Six, were published by private companies and the government left it entirely to each school to prescribe whatever textbooks the teachers concerned or the headmaster decided. In the case of aided schools that is, non-government schools that received government grant, it could be the management that decided the textbooks. As stated above, it was only the English textbook for Form Six that was published by the government and it used to be printed at the Government Press. Until the Second World War, this textbook used to be changed every year but after the war started, due to shortage of paper this textbook continued to be used for three consecutive years.

The other textbooks published by private publishing companies would be submitted by the publishers to the Textbook Committee constituted by the government for its approval. After getting them approved by the Committee which ensured that these books covered the syllabuses of each class, all those publishing houses would send specimen copies of their publications to various schools for getting them prescribed by those schools. In government schools, as already stated, textbooks were prescribed by the teachers concerned and in aided schools it was usually the management that prescribed textbooks from among those specimen copies received from publishers. All those specimen copies finally found their way to the school library. The entire collection called the school library was kept under lock and key in a book case in the headmaster's office. In most schools those books – the few story books purchased with the annual grant and specimen copies of textbooks – were not issued to the children lest they got lost or damaged, which might invite adverse remarks about the library by the educational officer who went for annual inspection of the school. And that may lead to the denial of grant.

In the late 1930s and early1940s, however, some schools had a fairly good collection of children's books in their libraries, although the number of such books was not many. During the British period, needless to say, English

---

* Some schools, however, had switched to the regional language as medium of instruction by the late 1930s in the lower and upper p rimary classes (classes 1 to 8).

was the first language and the medium of instruction,* particularly in the secondary sections in all schools and so this collection was confined to books in English only. Of course, none of the Indian languages had begun to bring out children's books in those days but even the adult books in Indian languages seldom found a place in school libraries. These books, as stated above, were safely kept under lock and key and were beyond the reach of the children. In most schools, books from such collections were not issued out to the children and in fact, the children of those schools would not have even known that their schools had libraries.

In some schools, the headmaster or whoever was the English teacher would bring a pile of story books randomly picked up by him from that collection and calling out the names of pupils in the class one by one, distribute the books to each in the order in which the pile is kept. This was how it was in the school in which I was fortunate enough to study. This was the privilege of the students of Form Six (as class eleven was then called), which was the final year of secondary education in those days. The students had no choice; they were compelled so to say, to read whatever was given to them, whether they liked it or not. However, each child had to maintain a diary and he or she was expected to write down the title and author of the book, new words that he/she found in the book with their meanings from the dictionary and a brief summary of the story. This had to be done before the teacher distributed the books next time, which would be the date by which the students were asked to submit their diaries and return the books. The same set of books would be shuffled and redistributed and if any child happened to get the same book that was given to him earlier, he could get it changed.

Six years after our country attained independence, in 1953, the Government of India constituted a Commission under the Chairmanship of Dr. A. Lakshmanaswami Mudaliar to suggest the measures to be taken to improve the quality of school education. This Commission, for the first time in India emphasized the importance of good libraries and intelligent library service in schools. Pointing out the lack of either, the Commission deplored the miserable condition of libraries in schools at that time. The Report states, "We should like to state, at the outset, that in a large majority of schools, there are at present no libraries worth the name. The books are usually old, outdated, unsuitable, usually selected without reference to the students' tastes and interests. They are stocked in a few book shelves, which are housed in an inadequate and unattractive room." This was the condition of school libraries in the second half of the twentieth century!

After that the Commission turns its attention to the person who is in charge of the school library and comes down heavily on him and the consequences of having such a person in charge. According to the Commission, "the person in charge is often a clerk or an indifferent teacher who does this on a part-time basis and has neither a love for books nor knowledge of library technique. Naturally, therefore, there is nothing like an imaginative and well-planned library service which could inspire students to read and cultivate in them a sincere love of books." Going to the root of the problem, the Commission finds fault with the educators and the educational authorities. "What makes the situation particularly difficult is the fact that most teachers and headmasters and even the educational administrators and authorities do not realise how unsatisfactory this position is and, therefore, they have no sense of urgency in the matter. It is necessary, therefore, to give some idea of the school library as we conceive it" and the Commission suggested ways and means of developing both the library and library services in schools.

The Commission stresses that "the library must be made the most attractive place in the school" and explains in detail how it could be done. It then, speaks about the mode and criteria of selection of books for the library and what type of books are to be purchased. It also points out the necessity for the school library to have books for the teachers. The Commission's suggestion regarding reading guidance to pupils is based on the assumption that the schools have well-equipped libraries managed by professional librarians. The Commission also suggests that all public libraries should have children's sections which would supplement the resources of school libraries. Above all, it wants school libraries to be thrown open to the public in places where there are no public libraries. However, the commission does not overlook the problem of the paucity of children's books in Indian languages and hopes that the law of demand and supply would come into play if all schools have libraries and public libraries have children's sections. Most importantly, it also touches upon the need to relate classroom teaching with the school library.

These suggestions were simply ignored and a decade later, in 1966, the government constituted another Commission, under the chairmanship of Dr. D. S. Kothari for revamping school education. This Commission too gave some suggestions to improve library service in schools. While some of the suggestions as for example, those on socially useful productive work, were implemented to some extent, those on improving library services in schools were totally ignored.

This Commission recommended pooling of resources by a school complex comprising all schools in a village or a particular locality in a town. The resources would be in the central high school library from where the books are distributed by a van. In other words, the libraries of all schools, lower primary, upper primary and high schools, in a demarcated area would be served by a mobile library which draws from the library maintained by the centrally located high school and the collection would be replenished periodically, which may be weekly or fortnightly depending on the requirements of each school. The van may have to take daily trips as all schools would not want replenishments on the same day. This, no doubt, will save the schools in the area from investing on the infrastructure of libraries and the recurring expenditure on their maintenance. Whatever money is saved thus by the schools in the complex may be utilised for strengthening the collection and replacing the lost or damaged books. The idea is good as a stop gap arrangement.

The Commission has failed to realize that the school library is not just a reading centre as it earlier used to be; it is an information centre as well. The suggestion put forward by the Commission of a school complex maintaining a circulating library and sending out books from the central high school to schools in the neighbourhood does not fit in with this modern concept of the school library. As a stopgap arrangement, no doubt, this is a good proposition in the case of a developing country like India as it would save the capital expenditure on the construction of buildings for the library in each school. It would also considerably reduce the strain on the annual budget of each school because under this arrangement, books and periodicals for each school library are purchased out of the money pooled by a group of schools. The drawback is that it does not help children learn the use of library and books; nor does it help create library consciousness in them.

However, this will benefit schools and children only if a small change is made in the proposal put forward by this Commission. Every school should have its own core collection of reference books, which are not to be carted around from school to school on a periodical basis because the need for these books can arise at any time. We shall discuss this problem in chapter 3, 'Methods in the Library.' Anyway, neither the government at the centre nor the state governments have so far implemented Kothari Commission recommendations for improving library service in schools.

Surprisingly, both the Mudaliar and the Kothari Commissions have completely ignored the pre-primary schools or nurseries and kindergartens. The latter, no doubt, speaks of developing the physique, motor skills and good health habits, social attitudes, and good manners as well as of encouraging aesthetic appreciation, creative activity and stimulating intellectual curiosity. The nursery school has so far been a place where children play and learn jingles and rhymes in the forenoons and sleep in the afternoons. Wordsworth in his poem, "My Heart Leaps Up" writes:

My heart leaps up when I behold
A rainbow in the sky;
So was it when my life began;
So is it now I am a man;
So be it when I shall grow old;
Or let me die!

The child is father of the Man,

............"

When he says "the child is father of the Man," he means that a man's personality is formed when he is a child and he will have the same personality as an adult also.

The personality of a person is the sum total of his physical, intellectual, abilities like his attitudes, habits and so on. A habit created in a child dies hard and it is difficult for him or her to change or to rid himself/herself of his/her childhood habits. So love of books and reading habit should be instilled in children at a very early age and it is necessary to begin to acquaint a child with books as soon as he is two years old. This has to be done at home by the parents or an elder sibling and nursery schools should continue this process. But not a word is said about instilling a love of books and creating reading habits in pre-school children either in the Report of Mudaliar Commission or in that of Kothari Commission. Mudaliar Commission ignored it, maybe because it was focussed on secondary school education only but Kothari Commission was expected to give suggestions to improve the whole gamut of school education.

Little children of all countries – irrespective of their ethnicity, colour, tradition, or IQ – are enraptured by grandma's tales and they seldom go to sleep without listening to the yarns that their grandmas weave everyday. Those could be about the heroic acts of their ancestors, about the wars that gods and angels fought against demons or about benign fairies and elves that help children; those could be about a cunning fox that escaped the wrath of a lion by some trickery or about a faithful dog that saved his master's child from drowning. Many of grandma's tales may not be found in any book; most of them are spontaneous products of her own creativity. The number of tales in the repertoire of grandmas is incredibly unlimited.

It is this natural interest that children show in listening to grandma's tales, that parents and nursery schools should exploit to create in them an interest in books and reading. Instead of narrating instant stories as grandmas do, parents and nursery schools should read out to them stories from illustrated juvenile books. And when they read, they must show them the relevant pictures related to the story. A child's interest in books and reading has its own inherent momentum and once created, this momentum carries it forward. But it does not mean that the child should be left to himself; further fuel should be added to it and that is to be done in the kindergartens, primary and upper primary schools. It has been found that the age eight to ten is the best period to create in children an abiding interest in reading. We shall deal with this further in chapter 2, 'Aims of the School Library.'

It must be borne in mind that the "library is a growing organism" and to make the school library a useful instrument of education, it should be equipped with a good selection of books. That this question may not arise when the school library is automated and e-books replace printed books is a different matter that we shall discuss in chapter 5, 'Resources.' Anyway, such a situation may not arise in our country in the immediate future although to some extend, virtual library gives an indication. As it is, the initial grant and annual budgetary outlay for the library should be commensurate with the enrolment in the school. In one word, if the school library has to meet the curricular and non-curricular demands of the school, the grant should be generous enough to meet the expenditure for buying new books and for replacing the lost or damaged books. Some of the books may have to be rebound and the expenditure for this should come under the budgetary head of maintenance of the school.

The different categories of books, that the school library should have, are dealt with in chapter 5, 'Resources.' Those have the printed documents that the library collection should have. Apart from these it is essential for the school library to have audio-visual aids like globe, film projectors, DVD players (audio and video cassettes are become obsolete today and possibly even DVDs may become obsolescent in the not too distant future), radio, television and slides. It is desirable to have a collection of realia in the library. The librarian and the teachers should help collect and label specimens of various stones, fossils, soil, wood and such other objects that may be of use in teaching. All these must be properly arranged and displayed in glass-topped cases in the library. Some librarians disapprove of this on the ground that library is not a museum. True; the library is not a museum. But these should not be viewed as exhibits in a museum; these must be regarded as visual aids.

A school library can be organised basically in four ways.

1. School Library: The only library with access to students and staff of the entire school managed by a professional librarian;
2. Central library and class libraries;
3. Central library and departmental libraries;
4. Central library, class libraries and departmental libraries.

School library : One library that caters to the entire

school and is the most desirable system from an educational, economic and administrative point of view. If the school has kindergarten classes as well as higher secondary classes, this library would cater to the higher secondary classes too but not to the kindergarten classes, which will have class libraries. However, the purchase and processing of books and other resources for the kindergarten would be the task of the school library. To have a single library serving the entire school is ideal because the students get a real experience of working in a library in a typical library atmosphere. The entire wealth of the library resources being in one place, this arrangement will help children get the books that are suited to their intellectual capacity, tastes and interests and the library will be able to achieve its educational aims, which we shall discuss in the next chapter, 'Aims of the School library.' This also helps obviate some drawbacks that the other possible organizational structures that are listed above, have. For example, if all books are in the school library, any teacher or student can freely and rightfully ask for any book at any time during working hours of the school even if the librarian is engaged in technical work. And the school library will remain open half an hour both before and after the working hours of the school.

Central library and class libraries. The school librarian would be technically in charge of these libraries and the class libraries would be managed by the class teachers. Under this system each class will have about fifty to a hundred books that are comprehensible to and appropriate for the age group, that is books that are suited to their interests, tastes and intellectual level. However, these books could be periodically changed by sending them back to the central library and replacing them with some others from the central library and either the teacher in charge or/and the librarian shall select them. A core collection of dictionaries and desk encyclopaedias, however, may be kept in the class libraries permanently. This makes it convenient for the teacher(s) and students of the class to refer to if need be during the lesson instead of waiting for the period to give over, to go to the central library for the purpose. A point strongly in favour of this organisation is that the children are exposed to books all the time and that may tempt them to read and thus develop the reading habit. These books can be read sitting in the classroom or borrowed to be read at home.

Central library and departmental libraries. In this organization too the school librarian would be technically in charge of the libraries. The books that may be required by the teachers concerned and students to refer to, frequently, would be in the departmental libraries, of which the head of the department would be in charge. As in the case of class libraries, if the teachers desire, all or a few of these may be exchanged for some other books in the central library. Or, any other book(s) required by the teacher(s) may be transferred to the department(s) for a short period or permanently.

Central library, class libraries and departmental libraries. This system too has the same advantages that the central library-cum-class libraries organisation has. As in the earlier two types, the school librarian would be in charge of all these libraries. The departmental libraries which will have reference books related to the subjects only would be managed by the head of the department. The class teachers would be in charge of the class libraries, which will have fiction and popular non-fiction books. But under this system the central library becomes just a transit centre and a depository of unwanted books. At best, it is a reading room with a few newspapers and magazines. There is no *raison d'etre* for a professional librarian and he becomes superfluous. So instead of the school/central library there could be a small reading room with a few newspapers and magazines and a few shelves of books rejected by teachers, managed by a clerk who will take care of correspondence pertaining to the library like ordering books, sending reminders to publishers or vendors and for defaulted magazines. This does not help achieve the educational objectives that are expected of a school library. This system is worse than any other pattern of school library organization and is to be abjured.

Some schools may prefer to have four libraries, one for each section:

1. Lower Primary School library
2. Upper Primary School library
3. Secondary School library
4. Higher Secondary School library

The school librarian will be in charge of the higher secondary school library which serves as the central library as well as in charge of all other libraries. The other sectional libraries will be managed by the class teachers of classes five, eight and ten. respectively or any other teacher of that section. Instead, certain schools may choose to have two libraries with the lower and upper primary schools having one library and the other two sections, one library.

In spite of some advantages, whatever be the combination, the disadvantages of fragmentation of the school library are more than the advantages. First of all, experience has shown that reading interests of children of classes five and six as also eight and nine, often overlap. Hence if books for recreational reading are segregated, it would impede the development of gifted children of the lower classes. Similarly, retarded readers would be denied the books of their standard, when they go into the sixth and ninth classes. Secondly in most cases the teacher who is in charge of a library may consider it a burden thrust on him.

Besides, when the library is compartmentalised, the students and the staff will have access to the books of a particular library only and they are practically denied the use of books that are in the other libraries. Let alone borrowing books from other libraries, they may not be able to get even to refer to many encyclopaedias and other reference books when they need any of them. For example, if a biology teacher, more so a biology student working on a term paper, who wants to refer to a reference book that is in the library of chemistry department may feel delicate to ask for it when the teacher in charge of that library is taking a class or if the teacher is busy with some work like preparing question papers or evaluating answer papers. Hence, in all these combinations, several reference books may have to be duplicated causing an unnecessary drain on library funds; rather it is a waste of funds. This and the problem of students researching for projects and term papers could be overcome to some extent if all reference books are in the central library. Apart from all the defects of decentralisation of library in the school by fragmenting it and organising it as different exclusive units, the worst is the lack of attractiveness of the central library that acts as the school library. All good and interesting books will be in the various exclusive units and only the rejects will be in the central library. Hence children may not be interested in visiting the central library.

These exclusive libraries would not be open to the children at all times and the students would be able to get books only when the teachers concerned in charge are free to open the book cases and issue books. I said, *book cases*, because in these libraries books are kept under lock and key lest they get stolen or vandalized. This is another drawback of fragmentation. In all these libraries the books have to be kept under lock and key as all the time the teacher in charge may not be in the room where books are kept. So naturally the children would not be able to browse on the books that are in bookcases as they would be able to in the school library where books are stacked in open shelves which are accessible to the children any time during school hours.

Unfortunately, even today some of the schools that have libraries have refrained from adopting open access system and many school libraries that have opted for open access have framed rules that are inhibitive and effectively nullify the advantages of open access. Their justification is that such rules are necessary to prevent pilferage and vandalism. The schools that refuse to allow free access to book shelves in libraries also hold the possibility of pilferage and vandalism as reasons for keeping the children away from the shelves. These school authorities do not realise that browsing the library shelves helps children find books suitable for them, which otherwise they would not have come to know of. More importantly, apart from creating an interest in reading, exposure to books like that indubitably develops love for books in children. And to some extent that discourages vandalism of books.

However, there is no gainsaying the fact that open access system makes it easy for anti-social elements among the children to pilfer and vandalise books. There are several reasons for malpractices like pilferage and vandalism in school libraries. It has been observed that many a time, a child who has been reprimanded by the librarian for any misdemeanour, steals a book or damages one to spite the librarian, without realising that he is not harming the librarian but his school mates and many children who would be joining the school in coming years. Another child, attracted by the colourful pictures may pilfer the book but his interest in those pictures may later vanish and he might throw away or destroy the book without the knowledge of anyone lest he would be punished for stealing a library book. These are misdemeanours that are not rooted in any psychological maladies as for example kleptomania and such children cannot be regarded as problems.

Vandalism is inevitable both in children's as well as adult libraries whether they are open access or otherwise. It is not difficult to cut off pages or pictures from books that are checked out of a closed access library. A child may remove pictures or cut off a few pages from a book he has borrowed and no counter clerk or librarian would be able to find it because checking page by page, each book that is being returned is impossible. In open access libraries, a member may stealthily cut off from a book whatever pages he/she wants from behind a shelf when no one is nearby or watching him or her. It is not possible for the librarian to keep an eye on many children simultaneously. Even electronic warning system at the exit door will not be able to detect when a child goes out with a few pages in his pocket. Loss of books due to pilferage and vandalism is a price worth paying for, for the benefit that open access gives to children.

It is a sad commentary on the successive governments that even sixty years after India attained independence, the condition of libraries and library services in our schools has not improved as much as it should. The schools in our country even in most towns still lack adequate library facilities. If at all there are libraries in schools in the towns and cities of our country, there would be no professional librarians to manage them; nor would there be adequate number of books, let alone

2

Aims of the School Library

Unlike the public library, which is an independent unit and does not subserve any particular institution, the school library is an adjunct of the school and is constrained to support the educational programmes of the school. In other words, the school library programme has to be oriented to the curricular and co-curricular requirements of the school. The school library, thus, differs from all other types of libraries and has certain distinct features. The most important of these is that it is directed towards certain definite educational aims, which are, in the final analysis, as stated above, of the school itself. Not just that. The school library has to extend its services beyond the school campus and reach out to school drop-outs as well as those sections of population that are maginalised by the society of the area that the school serves.

The school library being, to use a cliché, the hub of school life, provides support to not only the curricular but also the co-curricular work in the school and if demanded, stretches itself to the extra-curricular activities of the children. The extra-curricular activities are children's personal interests like hobbies or whatever they are interested in other than those directly or indirectly related to the school curriculum. These, incidentally, help develop library consciousness in children who, consequently in later life are bound to utilise public libraries as well as academic libraries like the college, university and special libraries, as the case may be. The school library, thus, produces the clientele of all other types of libraries and is the pedestal on which the entire library movement in the country – why, in the world itself – stands.

All types of libraries, including the school library, are primarily reading centres, be it the traditional library or the electronic library of the future, the difference being, in the former printed books are read while in the latter e-books are read. What is it that constitutes 'reading'? Or what is the meaning of the word, 'read'? The dictionary gives many meanings for the word 'read.' Basically, reading is the process of identifying the letters of an alphabet which are the symbols representing phonemes or certain sounds, accepted by a certain group of people. But in the context in which we use it here, the word 'read' does not just mean identification of the letters of the alphabet but has a different connotation that is wider than what the meanings that dictionaries give. A person who is a literate may be able to read and comprehend a combination of letters given in a particular order, which is called a 'word.' No doubt, he is able to read a word because he has learnt to identify the different letters of the alphabet. When he finds, for example the name of a physician written on a board fixed in front of his house or his own name printed on his voter identity card, he reads it. And he is able to comprehend combinations of letters called words arranged in a sequence according to an accepted set of rules called grammar, conveying an idea. This sequence of words is called a sentence. And he reads comprehending the idea conveyed by the sentence.

But when we say library is a reading centre, the word 'reading' does not denote the mechanical aspect of the act of reading; it connotes that the visitors to the library use it as a place to get books to read for pleasure or for information. Whether they read it on the premises of the library or not is immaterial. However, a person who reads for information cannot be said to have developed the reading habit, which implies a compulsive desire of the person to read. Habit is any type of behaviour, good or bad, that a person acquires as a result of certain external stimulus or stimuli to which he or she is continually subjected. A habit can be good or bad. For example, we brush our teeth every morning as soon as we wake up. This is a good habit that we developed because of the stimulus to which we were forcibly subjected by our parents or guardians in our childhood. On the other hand, if a person influenced by his friends consumes alcoholic drinks every day in the evening after he comes out of office, over time he gets addicted to alcohol and feels uneasy if he does not get alcohol in the evening. He thus develops a bad habit. Habit is a tendency to act in a certain way under certain specific conditions and in course of time it gets ingrained in the person. It is, therefore, not easy to change a habit.

Needless to say, literacy which makes it possible for a person to read and write is the first step towards developing the reading habit. All literates can read but all those literates who read cannot be said to have acquired the reading habit. Many people read because reading is a necessity in the world today. They read, for example, to find out the destination of the bus they are boarding; they read advertisements, notices and signboards in front of shops. Many people read pamphlets and manifestoes of political parties and such other materials. Some persons necessarily read the user's manuals to learn how to operate gadgets that they have purchased or how to assemble an electronic device and many students refer to books and other printed documents to research a particular subject. A clerk in an office or an IAS/IPS officer cannot but read everyday the many files that he deals with; so also the other professionals like teachers, lawyers, doctors and law makers cannot carry out their work without reading. Seldom do we find a literate person who does not take at least a glimpse of the daily newspaper to find out what is happening in the world around and there are many who read newspapers daily without fail. All political workers and lawmakers are constrained to read to keep in touch with the developments in their State and the country as well as in the world at large.

Every school child is compelled to read his textbooks if he wants to secure a high score in the examination and when reading his textbook he may have to look up the dictionary to find the meaning of a word that he does not know. He has to read to find out the meaning. He cannot do his homework or assignments unless he reads and when doing his assignments he would have to refer to an encyclopaedia or other source books, which he reads. If he has a hobby, as for example philately, he would like to know what country has issued a stamp which he has got but which he had not seen earlier. And for this he refers to Stanley Gibbon's *Stamp Catalogue* or any other book that gives the information that he wants. He reads that. Or he may want to know more about the country, which has brought out a particular stamp that he has got, for which he has to read books about that country. Unfortunately, even many of the language and literature teachers of schools and colleges do not read any book except the prescribed textbooks, which they have to read for teaching.

All those persons who read nothing other than what are necessary to carry out their work or duties cannot be said to have developed the reading habit. They read because they cannot help reading them. Similarly, students who read only their textbooks and other supplementary material necessary for their examinations have not developed the reading habit. To these persons, reading is drudgery, for they do not enjoy reading those documents. The term 'reading habit' denotes the urge to read for pleasure and hence a person who has acquired the habit of reading regards reading not as drudgery or a chore but as a recreational activity. It is immaterial whether he reads fiction or non-fiction as long as he is reading it for pleasure. He enjoys reading it. To put it differently, a person who reads for pleasure is said to have developed the reading habit. These persons do not need any external pressure or inducements to read but this, as the term 'habit' indicates is not congenital. It is acquired as a result of external stimulus to which he is subjected or certain favourable conditions at home or/and at school, that are tantamount to stimuli to which he has been exposed.

This stimulus that creates reading habit in a person is 'books' and hence the imperative for a good library in every school. Not many homes in our country have collections of books, for which the elders are not to be faulted. Books are too expensive for most people to buy. Let alone those parents who are first or second generation literates or illiterates, many of those who are well-educated having post-graduate degrees, would not have developed the habit of reading for pleasure. Unfortunately, it is difficult to find a collection of books even in the homes of the affluent class, although in some houses of the affluent class, beautifully bound volumes can be seen arranged on carved wooden shelves kept as showpieces in sitting rooms. These are not meant to be read and children are not expected to browse, let alone read them, lest the books are begrimed! So the only place where most of the children in our country can freely see, smell, touch and read books other than their textbooks is the school library.

Hence the responsibility for introducing children to books devolves upon the school library. There are certain aims specific to library services in schools and it is imperative that librarians and teachers are aware of them. What are these aims? The primary and the most important of all, is to create in children a positive attitude towards books and inculcate the reading habit in them. However, it is the responsibility of not only the school librarian but also the teachers, particularly the language and literature teachers. Habit as we have seen already becomes ingrained and so if reading habit is created in a child, it becomes a part of his nature. Although after leaving the school at times when suitable books are not available, this habit may lie dormant in him but as soon as he gets some books or he is placed where books are available, the old habit would raise its head. And he reads.

But a good school librarian should not be content with instilling the reading habit. Along with instilling the reading habit, the school librarian has to guide each child's reading to help improve his reading taste and widen his reading interests. Reading habit, reading taste and reading interest are three aspects of general reading. Reading habit as you have already seen is the urge to read for pleasure and the quality of the books a person reads shows his reading taste, which may be good or bad while the area or the subjects that his reading covers may be said to be his reading interest, which may be wide or limited. The library cannot achieve these objectives unless the children visit the library. But a child who is not interested in reading will not step into the library of his own volition and so the school has to create a situation in which he or she is compelled to go to the library. So the co-operation of the school authorities as well as the entire faculty is imperative in fulfilling these objectives. This problem will be discussed in the next chapter when we deal with methods in the library. Suffice it to say here that every class should have a library period on the timetable when they come to the library.

These aims determine the style of functioning of the school library and distinguish it from all other types of libraries, which deal with and are expected to serve only those who visit those libraries. In other words, the aims of those libraries, even college libraries, are merely to provide a congenial atmosphere for their clientele and to help the readers to find the books they want or to retrieve the information they are seeking. The children's public libraries and adult public libraries that have juvenile sections may organise story reading sessions for the juvenile members that help develop reading habit in them. Nevertheless, these story reading sessions attract only those who are interested in them unless the librarian seeks the help of parents of all juvenile members to bring their children for these sessions. Whether the librarian of any children's library or public library in our country does this is a sixty-five million dollar question. And of course, it is not his responsibility; it is for the parents of the children concerned to take them to the story reading sessions. Leaving aside this activity of public libraries, all types of libraries including public libraries, other than the school library, are 'reactive' by which I mean they only to react to the demands of the clientele. And that is what they are expected to. No one who is not interested in reading would step into any public – adult or children's – libraries and the librarians of those libraries are not concerned with them.

Like the children's or adult public library the school library also caters to those children who are interested in reading and who visit the library without any coercion. But at the same time the school library is obliged to be proactive because the school library cannot be unconcerned with children who are not interested in reading and remain simply 'reactive.' It has definite educational aims, which make it incumbent upon the school librarian to coax the reluctant and reticent children to read. It is these educational aims that make the school library significantly different from the children's public library and it is that which compel the school library to be proactive. This, as stated above, is necessitated by its clientele and its approach to the clientele and it is this that differentiates the school library from the children's public library. The children's public library serves only those who have the reading habit and go to it whereas the school library is concerned equally, if not more, with the children who have not developed the reading habit as well as those who are retarded readers. Those children are, therefore, not interested in reading and do not go to the library of their own volition. Unlike the children's public library, the school library is also expected to help children who have developed the reading habit widen their reading interest as well as refine their reading taste.

The other objectives, which are specific to the school library, rest chiefly on the shoulders of the librarian. The first and the most important of these objectives, is to teach the children how to conduct themselves in the library. It is in the school library that children, who are the prospective clientele of all other types of libraries, learn the "Dos and

Don'ts" in a library. This, in one word, is ethic, to be precise, the library ethics. The library ethics is not taught by giving a couple of lectures but is instilled in children unobtrusively over time. Incidentally, this should be one of the aims of the children's public library also but in instilling library ethics, stress should be placed on the positive – the "Dos" rather than on the "Don'ts." We shall come back to this in the next chapter.

Another objective of the school library, which perhaps is redundant in the case of virtual library or in the not too distant future when digital library replaces the traditional library of printed documents, is to familiarise the pupils with library techniques. These techniques comprise basically the system of classification that the library follows and the structure of the card catalogue, whether classified or dictionary type. The children should be given an idea of whatever is the classification system used in the library. If the library has adopted the Dewey Decimal System, which in my opinion is the most suited for children's libraries (and even for all other types of libraries), the children should be acquainted with the general pattern of the system. Similarly, they must be trained to use the catalogue – both classified and dictionary. If they have a basic idea of the classification system, the classified catalogue will not pose any problem. But they must have a good grasp of the alphabetical order to use the dictionary catalogue without any difficulty. So they must be taught the alphabetical order in the primary classes and this can be done with the help of word games, a couple of examples of which are given in the Appendix.

In order to familiarise the students with the classification system, as many copies as required of the ten Classes, ten Divisions and ten Sub-Divisions of knowledge as conceived by Dewey, if Decimal system is the one used in the library, must be taken and put up on the notice board in the library as well as on all other bulletin boards in the school including the staff room(s). One copy must be pasted on a cardboard and kept on the catalogue cabinet. The structure of this classification system must be imparted to them in the course of helping the children to find the source books when they come to research or when they come to look for books to be taken out for recreational reading. However, some librarians may prefer otherwise – to teach classification system as other subjects are taught in the classroom. We shall deal with both these methods in detail in the next chapter. It is, therefore, left to the librarian concerned to decide how to acquaint the children with classification system.

The school librarian has a duty to the faculty also as one of the objectives of the school library is to help the teachers improve themselves professionally and academically. The school library, in its preoccupation with the children should not, therefore, ignore the teaching community, which too constitutes an equally important segment of its clientele. The school library should serve the teachers as a virtual centre of continuing education that helps them keep themselves abreast of the latest developments in the disciplines that they are teaching as well as in pedagogy. So the members of the teaching faculty have to be fed regularly with information about the resources available in the library pertaining to the literature of their areas of specialization. Needless to say, in the final analysis it is the students who benefit by this.

Apart from keeping the teachers informed of the resources that the library has and latest additions related to their respective areas of interest, all articles that appear in journals regarding latest developments in various disciplines, especially sciences, the librarian must draw the attention of the teacher(s) concerned to the those articles. Any development in related subjects reported in newspapers also should be brought to the notice of the teachers concerned. For example, if a report in any newspaper or an article in any magazine appears about some new archaeological finds of the period of Ashoka or that of the Mughals that have been unearthed by archaeologists, it should be brought to the notice of the history teacher. Similarly, if a good critique of a well-known litterateur is published in a magazine, the librarian should draw the attention of the teacher concerned to it. If the school has a Xerox machine, a photocopy of the article may be given to the teacher who might be interested in it.

It would be a wise investment to set apart a certain percentage of the library budget for the purchase of books and periodicals solely for the use of the teaching staff. The library must subscribe to two or three educational journals like the *Journal of Indian Education* published by the National Council for Educational Research and Training, *Journal of the Indian Academy of Applied Psychology* and any other such periodicals. Articles and news on the educational policies of the government of India and various state governments appearing in daily newspapers should be clipped and put up on the bulletin board in the staff room. If the school has necessary funds, it is desirable to subscribe to the *Secondary Education* published in the United Kingdom. As recommended by the Mudaliar Commission, every school library should have a good selection of books on education and pedagogy. It is also imperative to subscribe to one or two journals pertaining to library science/services for the librarian to keep in touch with latest developments in the field, in which the impact of electronic revolution is bringing about unprecedented changes.

The first and the most important of the aims of school library, is instilling the reading habit in pupils. Reading habit is not inherited; it is an acquired habit. As Aidan Chambers wrote, "Readers are made, not born. No one comes into the world already disposed for or against words in print." There is no gainsaying the fact that parents are the first teachers of a child and introducing books to children is the bounden duty of the parents. It has been found that freshmen in the lower kindergarten or class one to whom, parents – mother or father – had been reading out stories have a better sense of language, respond better in the class than those whose parents had not exposed them to books at home during their pre-school years. The former group evinces a keen interest in mastering the mechanics of reading and articulates even difficult words clearly. Quick on the uptake, those children soon learn to recite and easily memorise rhymes. I have observed that generally those who had been introduced to books at an early age not only take to recreational reading of their own volition but have an edge over their less fortunate peers in studies.

The problem is that in our country, as stated above, not many houses have books at home and if they have and even if both the parents of the children of lower and upper middle class families are educated, they do not find the time to read out books to their children. Early morning they go to work and in the evening when they come back they have household chores to attend to. Yet, there are several such families where parents do somehow find the time to share with their children the pleasure of reading books. Child psychologists agree that the most impressionable period of a child's life is the first five years and the rate of development of a child's intelligence is far greater during that period of a child's life than at any time in later years.

So the foundation for love of books must be laid at the

preschool stage. But there is another impediment today. These days baby soothers, rattles and other toys used earlier to pacify toddlers when they cry and when they have tantrums have all become obsolete. Their place has been taken up by television. When the baby cries or when a two-year old refuses to eat, the mother puts on the television. That does help then, but the parents are unconsciously harming them.

Children are naturally inclined to play and children born of lower and upper middle class families and affluent class parents who can afford a television, spend a bulk of their childhood watching the television. This adversely affects their physical fitness and health; worse still they become addicted to television. The addiction, naturally, persists in them and is an impediment to developing the reading habit. Besides they spend a large part of their time watching TV programmes, neglecting their studies also. It is, no doubt, a good recreation but not if the children spend all their free time on it without even going to play as it is happening today.

The idiot box has thus become a hindrance to the child's intellectual and physical growth. And left to them, children ignore programmes that have educational value and prefer to watch only certain reality shows that encourage some of the basest elements in human nature and those that glorify violence; or they switch on some soap operas. Let the children watch any programme meant for children on TV or play computer games but not all the time. It is up to the parents to monitor what they watch and ensure that they do not get glued to the TV.

However, television cannot be condemned altogether. There are many programmes that help enlarge their general knowledge. The fault lies with the parents who do not consider it their responsibility to create a taste in their children for such programmes. They do not guide the children and try to develop an interest in the children to watch some educative or informative programmes. The parents must insist on their children sit with them when they watch news telecast daily and after that discuss the news for about five or ten minutes. The time spent on this is worthwhile. In a democratic country like India it is necessary that children grow up, aware of what is happening in the country and in the world. That will make them good and informed citizens.

And now enters the computer which too is an excellent means of recreation and education but as in the case of the TV, it depends on how it is made use of by children. By the time a child of affluent class masters the alphabet and learns to read, he or she finds a new and interesting toy in the computer and spends his leisure time playing computer games. It has been found most children who have computers at home use it for recreational purposes, all the time playing computer games, which become addictive. Or, they spend a lot of time on it aimlessly browsing or slyly visiting pornographic web sites. Most parents do not care what their children are doing with the computer and in fact they are ignorant of the harmful effect it has on children.

At the same time it must be understood that the computer is a very useful instrument of education. A computer with internet connection, in fact, is virtual library where they can access encyclopaedias, dictionaries and source books on all subjects as well as periodicals on-line apart from works of imaginative literature of many authors of the classic and modern times that are now in the public domain. Above all, it is the best source of information and students doing assignments, researching a project or working on a term paper will find it extremely useful. The greatest advantage is that it is accessible all the time unlike the school and public libraries which can be made use of only during the working hours of those libraries. Unfortunately, computers today are too expensive to buy for a vast majority of our countrymen, a large percentage of which are denied even school education despite the Constitutional amendment making education a fundamental right. Anyway, that is beside the point.

As stated above, both television and computer are good educational tools but they are seldom used by children for educational purposes and it is the responsibility of the parents to persuade the children to use the television and computer beneficially. But, the parents do not seem to realise this. The situation will hopefully change when computers become a part and parcel of teaching and learning process in schools.

There is a general impression that the advent of television and subsequently the computer has impinged on the reading time of children resulting in the waning of reading habit. But I do not subscribe to this view. The tremendous interest evinced by children in Harry Potter series disproves the theory that TV and computer have turned the children away from books and dampened their interest in reading. Besides, statistics tell us that sale of children's books has not been showing any downward trend; on the other hand the demand for children's books has been growing steadily. Anyway, as stated already, it is the duty of the parents to expose their children to books at an early stage in their lives. It will go a long way in preventing them from getting addicted to the electronic devices. But the fact that today books are too expensive to buy even for an upper middle class family, let alone the lower middle class is the problem.

The solution to this problem lies in taking advantage of the local public library. Public libraries do not levy any membership fee; there is only a nominal *refundable* deposit to be paid. The parents should take library membership so that they can borrow suitable children's books from the library and read them out to their children in order to instil in them an interest in reading. And they should also make their children members of the public library as soon as they are admitted in the school, whether the school has a library or not. The school library will not be open during vacations when the children can make use of the public library. Unfortunately, there are not enough public libraries in towns and villages to meet the demands of the fast growing population of literates and the educated in our country. In most parts of our country, there are many villages that do not have a library. In places there are no public libraries, the school library should be kept open for an hour or two on week days during the vacation for the benefit of the students. The librarian must be paid a special allowance for this extra work he would be doing.

Another difficulty is, in many families the parents are either first generation or second generation literates and they themselves have not developed the reading habit because the schools in which they had studied would not have had a library. Several of them may be (elementary or high) school drop outs too. Naturally, therefore, they would not be interested in buying books and having a collection of books in the house even if they could afford it; nor would they think of buying juvenile books for their children to read. As stated earlier, a vast majority of children in our country see or touch a book only when they join the pre-school and so it is the responsibility of pre-school/ kindergarten teachers to introduce books to children and create in them a love for books. This presupposes good library in every pre-school/kindergarten.

In fact, it is here that the foundation for reading habit in children should be laid. However, let alone what may be called a library, few pre-schools which have mushroomed in our country in recent years have even a small collection of any kind of books. The depressing aspect is that many of those who run these institutions are uneducated and have no concept of education whatsoever; hence they do not think it necessary for pre-schools to have a library. Some of the pre-schools are run in ill-ventilated, dingy rooms with one teacher who is generally a person without requisite qualifications, teaching both the lower and upper kindergarten classes. It is, therefore, imperative that every State government bring in a legislation regulating pre-schools and formulate rules like those governing elementary and secondary schools.

In the past, the school library was looked upon as only a reading centre, but gradually it has become an information centre too where children go to collect information on the topic they are researching or interested in. So unlike in olden days, the school librarians emphasise not just on reading but on both reading and research – more on the latter than on the former. It is not enough schools have well-equipped libraries with a good selection of books that suits the various age groups and tastes of children; they must be used. The test of the pudding is in its eating and the test of any type of library is in the use made of it by the clientele, which in the case of the school library are the children and the faculty.

The school library, as stated above, is expected to be proactive. In specific terms it should not simply wait for the juvenile clientele to come to the library whenever they are in a mood or find time to visit the library. All children may not have the inclination to read but many of them, if they are exposed to good books, take to recreational reading of their own volition as soon as they master the mechanics of reading, Nevertheless, if left without a little compulsion, they may rather go out and play or waste their time in idle talk with their classmates while some may just laze away their time. The librarian should convince the headmaster and the teachers of the necessity to make it imperative for children to use the library and persuade them to have the school programme so oriented that all children are constrained to visit the library.

The first step towards this is to provide on the timetable one library period in a week for every class. That will make the children of every class to go to the library during that period, whether they like it or not. Some children, for example may not be interested in a particular subject, yet they are compelled to be in the class when that subject is taught. It may be argued that a minimum percentage of attendance is made mandatory to ensure that they learn the subject in which they have to take an examination at the end of the year and secure the minimum percentage of marks to be promoted to the next class. But no examination is held to test if a child had read certain specified books; nor would anyone be denied promotion if he or she does not step into the school library, let alone read books. However, today no sensible person would deny the importance of creating the reading interest in children. When the class comes to the library during the library period, it is up to the school librarian to spot out children who are reluctant readers and get them interested in reading books. The librarian should establish a rapport with each child, especially the reticent children. He should speak to the children as a friend – be friendly but not 'chummy' – and in the process try to understand what type of book each of them would enjoy.

No doubt, creating reading habit in children, who are not inclined to, is a daunting task and teachers cannot wash their hands of this responsibility. They, particularly language and literature teachers, can help considerably in creating the reading habit in children. So in order to be successful in this, it is desirable that the librarian and the teachers join hands. This is dealt with briefly in the next chapter and in detail in my book, *Library Services for Children*.

3

Methods in the Library

As pointed out in chapter 1, 'School Library — Its Rise and Organisation,' the objective of schools in India prior to independence was to train children for clerical work. But since India attained independence, the situation changed and that called for a change in the objectives of schools. The school is no more a factory for producing *en-masse* anglicised Indian clerks as it had been during the British period but has become an institution imparting real education. The present curriculum and syllabus drawn up by the NCERT/SCERT and various Boards of Examination like the CBSE and ICSE reflect the changed objective of the school education in our country.

Nevertheless, the weakness of school education in our country lies in the *teaching method*. The methodology of pedagogy needs to be overhauled thoroughly; more stress has to be given to investigative learning than, to use a cliché, on chalk and talk method of teaching. The bottom line is that the teacher must refrain from depending solely on the textbook and dictating notes. The children should be encouraged to research instead of confining themselves to their textbooks and the notes dictated by the teacher. The teacher should give the children assignments, projects and term papers that cannot be done without referring to reference books that are in the school library or the public library. Or to put it differently, the teacher should give the children assignments, projects and term papers that would compel them to look beyond the two covers of their textbooks. They must be forced to go to the school library or/and public library and refer to some source books on the subject concerned.

This may be called library-centred teaching, which calls for a well-equipped library managed by a full-time professional librarian in every school. This could have been put into practice if the recommendations of the Mudaliar Commission had been implemented. On the other hand, the recommendations of the Kothari Commission for improving library services, in effect positively preclude the adoption of library-centred teaching because this method presupposes a well-equipped library managed by a full-time professional librarian. Deficiencies, if any, of reference section would be compensated if the library has at least one computer with internet connection.

The distribution of books to a group of schools from a central pool by mobile libraries as envisaged by the Kothari Commission can certainly help in the sphere of literature meant for general reading. But these circulating libraries cannot serve effectively as information centres where reference books and materials other than books as for example the computer, are to be made available on demand at short notice. It is likely that more than one school may need a particular reference book at the same time for the students to carry out assignments or projects. It is impractical for and unrealistic to expect schools to co-ordinate students' research work if library-centred teaching method were to be adopted in all schools. Besides, if a teacher wants to refer to an encyclopaedia before starting on a new topic, to clear some doubt he or she has, it may not be available in the school library; the required book may be in another school where the students are working on an assignment on some topic that requires this reference book. And there may not be more than one copy of many of the informational books in the pool because those books are usually quite expensive and if more copies are to be purchased the very purpose of the system of circulating libraries is defeated.

The weakness of this system, thus, stands revealed when situations like these arise. Such situations would, doubtless, arise quite often when, as expected, the schools bury the present method of teaching based on textbooks and blackboard and adopt library-centred method. The books for mobile libraries should therefore be confined to the sphere of general reading material but even this may be treated as a transitional measure only. The sooner each school has a library of its own, the better. If the books of fiction are in the shelves of the school library, the children would get to browse upon them, get interested and thus develop the reading habit. But it is seldom and that too for a short while when the mobile library visits the school that the children get an opportunity even to have a glimpse of those books, let alone browsing.

Apart from the resources, in order to facilitate library-centred teaching the teachers should be encouraged to take their classes to the library for research and this could begin at the latest in class five or six. However, the teachers should bear in mind that the accommodation in the library is limited and there are classes coming to the library during library periods. The library may not be able to accommodate more than one class at a time. In order, therefore, to avoid any clash with another class, the teachers who want to take their classes to the library for research should make prior arrangement with the librarian, who can, then, prevent overcrowding in the library.

The teachers and the librarian should cooperate and work in tandem in relating classroom work with the library. They, both the teacher and the librarian must realise that classroom and the school library are not mutually exclusive but that the library is extended classroom. The teacher must, therefore, plan his lesson in such a way that it overflows into the library and whatever is briefly explained or left unsaid must be given as home work in the form of assignments that should compel the children to go to the school library and refer to resources other than textbooks. They may also browse the internet and collect relevant materials. The teacher or/and the librarian may suggest the books that they can refer to in the library and also tell them the web sites that are likely to give them the information that they are looking for. The librarian and the teacher should help the children find the books that the teacher suggests. This would help children learn on their own and would stand in good stead when they go to college where they cannot expect spoon feeding as some school teachers tend to do.

During this 'period in the library' as distinct from 'library period' the teacher who sends the children to research should necessarily accompany them to the library. So the period in the library is not for the teacher to take rest; in fact, taking the children to the library for researching an assignment for example or on group work on a project involves more work for the teacher than teaching in the class. First of all he must acquaint himself with the books that the library has on the topic he proposes to give for the project, for which he may have to spend a considerable time in the library for a few days prior to it. Even if he/she is taking the children to do an assignment he has to go to the library with the children to supervise. He has also to give some thought to split into various aspects the topic to be given to each child or group of children for research.

To begin with, what we call home work may be given as assignments pertaining to the lesson being taught in the class and it should not be difficult for a child of class five to do this. This doubtless may make most children, the average and above average students, go deeper into the subject. But the below average children would not be able to cope with this work. In order to avoid this problem, some teachers form groups mixing the brighter and weaker children and give assignments or projects to each group. But it has been found that the brighter ones in the group do all the work while the weaker children hang around and simply copy what the others have written. It is, therefore, advisable to avoid the system of group work. So the teacher who presumably must have identified such children should go to the library and help them out. After doing one or two assignments with the help of the teacher they will learn to do the work by themselves. They may be slow in completing the work but the teacher should appreciate their difficulty and condone the delay, making sure that they complete the assignment and submit.

Once the children learn the technique of research they must be given individually some small projects not directly related – but preferably collateral – to the lesson, which can be completed in one period. For example, if the class is being taught ancient civilisations, the students could be asked to write individually on any of the tribes of India in about a page. The next step is a class project on a topic. This topic may be split into several subject heads and each subject may be given to a group of five or six children to work on. Group work is now possible because by now the backward students would have mastered the technique of research and would take an active interest in the work. All these when put together would form a sort of a monograph. If the lesson being taught is Rabindranath Tagore's *Cabuliwallah*, topics for projects, for example, could be, (1) the Afghan tribes, (2) a critique of the story, (3) a brief account of Tagore's life, (4) Tagore and India's Freedom Movement, (5) Tagore as a litterateur, (6) Tagore as a painter, (7) Santiniketan, (8) Nobel and Nobel Prize. Assuming that the strength of the class is forty, the teacher may divide the class into eight groups of not more than five children in each and give each group a topic as suggested above connected with the story to work on. If the class has more than forty children, the teacher may think of a few more related topics like 'A short account of the history of Afghanistan' or 'A short note on any other Indo-Anglian writer.' Students of classes seven and eight would not find this difficult; on the other hand, they will find the work quite interesting. This will make learning a pleasure and the teacher will see them bubbling with enthusiasm.

Desirably, the teacher who goes to the library with the children for working on their assignments should, along with the librarian, help the children find source books that give the necessary information. Neither the teacher nor the librarian need go round the library and pick out the books for them from the shelves but tell them what books in the library would give the information they are looking for and how they could find those books. In other words, this is the right time to acquaint them with the classification system and the intricacies of the catalogue. So the students would be well versed in the use of books and library by the time they step into the secondary school.

The teacher would now find that the students have gained sufficient experience in research work and he could give them term papers to work on. These papers may be preferably on any topic directly connected with the syllabus or even if it is not so, it should not be totally divorced from the syllabus. The teacher need not give the topic. It is better each student is given the liberty to choose whatever topic pertaining to the subject concerned he or she is interested in. However they must be told that it should be some topic within the syllabus and the teacher can give a few topics as examples or a list of topics from which each one could choose what he or she desires to work on. The teacher can tick off the topic a child has chosen so that the same is not taken up by another child. The students may submit the papers for evaluation any time during the term. They must be told that a certain percentage of the marks that they score in the term papers would be added on to the marks in the annual examination so that they take the work seriously. When a class is asked to write a term paper for the first time, the teacher should brief them on how to organise a term paper and instruct them on note taking. Nevertheless, many children may approach the librarian to help them out. So the librarian will have to tell them how to proceed with the work of writing a term paper.

The student must be asked to choose the subject and choosing a subject is no doubt very important. The student should think of a subject that interests him and not anything that he thinks would be easy to work on. Before deciding on the subject, he should also check up with the librarian if he would get necessary references in case he chooses that subject. Suppose the topic chosen is 'Indus Valley Civilisation' after making sure that sufficient material on the subject would be available in the school library. For more information, the students should be encouraged to go to the public library, if necessary. First of all he must do some background reading on the subject, for which the best source is encyclopaedias. That will give him an idea as to what he should focus on in his paper as for example the period in which and the area where the civilisation flourished, the archaeological finds and so on. Now his problem is the sources from which he can retrieve the information and how to find them. The books in the library in which this information is given can be found out with the help of the catalogue. There could also be some clippings and pictures on it in the clippings file. That will help him to prepare a bibliography.

He can now start taking down notes. It is desirable the librarian teaches the students the technique of note taking. If this is left to the teachers, there is a possibility of the students getting confused as each teacher may teach a different method. After all, there is no specific way of note taking. The similarity between classification and note taking is striking and the librarian being an experienced classifier the technique of note taking comes natural to him as the subject under study has to be split into heads and subheads, which is akin to the classification schedule.

After taking down notes on these subjects he should make a draft of the essay, on completion of which he must revise to correct any spelling or grammatical errors that would have crept in. Now a fair copy can be made. It should have the title page with his name and date as well as the name of the teacher and the subject. Some boys may like to write the name of the school also. The title page is followed by the table of contents, and the text that is, the essay. In this case, there will be the map of the region, a map of India to show position of the Indus Valley in relation to the rest of India and some pictures of the archaeological finds.

These may be attached as 'Appendix.' The bibliography comes last unless there is an index which some may like to provide. It would be good to have an index if the student has the time to prepare one and the librarian should tell him how to prepare the index. If he has a computer at home and knows to use it, all this work would be very easy.

In order to make it easy for the students to find out the books and information for working on assignments, projects and term papers, it is imperative for the students to have a basic knowledge of the classification system and cataloguing. But it is not these alone in which the librarian has to instruct the students. Given below in the form of a syllabus is a list of those that the students have to be taught to make them use books and library effectively by the time they go into class nine.

Unit 1	Initiation
Unit 2	Library Ethics
Unit 3	Alphabetisation (Please see Appendix)
Unit 4	About the book
Unit 5	Dictionaries
Unit 6	Encyclopaedias
Unit 7	Other Reference Books
Unit 8	Card Catalogue
Unit 9	Classification System
Unit 10	Bibliography
Unit 11	Note Taking
Unit 12	Appraising the Literary Value of books

Although this list looks like a syllabus of one of the subjects in the curriculum, these may be imparted to the students informally and unobtrusively. I do not personally agree with those librarians who suggest that this is to be taught as a subject *pre se* setting apart a few library periods for it at the appropriate stage. It would be counterproductive as the children would find it quite boring and it is doubtless a drab subject for a person who does not intend to take up the profession of librarianship. In my opinion the librarian must make it possible for children to imbibe some of these (Units 1 to 3) at the lower primary school level, at times instilling it verbally in the erring individual at any opportune moment in a friendly way.

It is desirable to impart the techniques to the children when they come to the library during library periods or any time for borrowing books and for study and research so that they learn these unconsciously. The children who look for interesting books to read usually browse through books in the shelves and pick up one that they think would interest them. They know from their experience where or in which shelves, for example, books of fiction or those on biography are kept and as soon as they enter the library, they make a beeline for those shelves. But if one of those children goes to the public library to find some book that he needs, he gets lost not knowing in which shelves the books on the required subject can be found. There are, no doubt, guide cards indicating the shelves in which books on different subjects are kept but to find out if a book by a particular author is in the library or what all books of a particular author are there, he will have to go to the shelves and look through the titles of all the books displayed in the relevant shelves. After all that, if the book is really in the library but has been borrowed by some other member, he may think that the book he wants is not in the library.

The catalogue helps the reader avoid such situations. If he consults the catalogue he would know if the book by the author that he looks for is in the library and if it is, in which shelf it is kept. He also comes to know from the catalogue what other books by that author are in the library and also what other books on the subject are available in the library. Even if he knows only the title of the book the catalogue tells him whether the library has the book or not. The catalogue also gives him further details about the book. For example, he is able to know from the catalogue in which year that particular copy was brought out and what edition of the book is that copy. The catalogue also tells him if a later edition of the book is available in the library. It is possible that the topic that he is researching is also dealt with in several other books that are in the library and that information also he would be able to get from the catalogue through cross references.

So when a boy comes to look for a book to take home to read or to do an assignment the librarian should not miss the opportunity. He must introduce the child to the intricacies of the card catalogue. If, however, the catalogue is computerised, the boy must be told how to find from it the information about the book that he wants even if he does not know the name of the author or the exact title. It is enough he knows a key word or two of the title or the name of the author to find out all the information about the book from a computerised catalogue. Apart from all the information that a card gives, he will also know from the computerised catalogue, if the book that he wants is on loan and if so when it is due. The computerised catalogue will also tell him if there are any reservations for the book. And by typing out the name of the subject he will be able to find out what all books on that subject are available in the library. This opportunity may be also availed of to acquaint the student with the classification system used in the library. However, a brief introduction is enough and there is no need to teach him about the classification system in detail. And all this must be done unobtrusively.

The student who comes to research his assignment or project would naturally go for reference books first. That is the time to introduce him to the various reference books that are in the library. At that time, the student may be shown different parts of a book and told how useful they are when researching. He can find out from the table of contents the scope of the book and what each chapter deals with. The index will help him find the pages in which the information he wants is discussed. So he does not have to read the entire book to collect the information but read only the relevant pages.

When printed books are replaced by e-books completely and books could be accessed on the computer Units 4 to 10 would become redundant. At the rate at which electronic field is developing and the popularity of e-books is growing, this is likely to happen in all languages of the world within this century. Anyway, till then, familiarity with the classification system that is used in the library and the structure of the catalogue is essential for the children to enable them to access the material that they seek in the library.

The reason for giving this in the form of a syllabus is that some school librarians prefer instructing students in library ethics, use of books, library techniques and so on formally as a subject. It is possible to go through the entire course in six periods of forty minutes each. However, it is too difficult for children in the primary classes to comprehend all these units. At the same time it is not desirable to wait for the children to reach the high school for teaching them, all these; nor are all these to be taught at the upper primary school level. But then the question arises at what stage, teaching of these could begin. If the librarian decides to teach this as a subject in itself, it is advisable to spread out these through lower primary and upper primary schools so that by the time the children come to the secondary school they will be well versed in using library and books for study and research. Unit 12 may be left for the secondary school stage.

The librarians who prefer to instruct the students in these soon after the children are admitted in class one may follow a schedule. In that case, the units could be clubbed together as follows:

Lower Primary classes

One period for Units 1

One period for Unit 3

Upper Primary classes

One period for Units 4 to 7

Two periods for Units 8 to 10

One period for Unit 11

Secondary School classes

Unit 12 [This cannot be taught as a subject. The Librarian should organise a literary club for this purpose. This is explained below.]

It is too difficult for children in the primary classes to comprehend all these units. The first three Units (Initiation; Library Ethics; and Alphabetisation) may be taught in the lower primary classes itself. When freshmen come to the library for the first time during the library period the librarian must take them round the library telling them where each category of books are kept and showing them the catalogue and other equipment like the computer(s) in the library. It is at the school library that library ethics are instilled into young minds but library ethics cannot be taught as for example teaching the branch of philosophy called 'ethics' in one period or in a year; it should continue till the student passes out of the school. It is seen, for example that children in their 'teens tend to forget that they are not expected to talk loudly in the library. That is the stage when they infringe many of the ethical principles that had been dinned into them since they first stepped into the library at the age of five.

However, it is necessary to commence teaching them some of these ethical principles in the primary school itself. They are, as stated above, Units 1 to 3. Here they are taught to read silently and to talk, *if necessary*, in undertones as they are expected to in a library. Here they may be shown how to take out from and replace in the shelf without damaging the books they want. They are told to place the index finger on top of the book, press down and pull outward, taking care not to damage the spine of the book in the process. They are shown the right way to turn the pages of a book and are persuaded to eschew such unhygienic habit like wetting their fingers with saliva, which many adults have. The desirability of using a book-mark instead of indulging in the practice that almost amounts to malpractice, of folding the top corner of the page is brought home to them. They are made to realise the damage that may be caused to the book if placed face downwards on the table. They are also made to understand how a book gets spoiled if used as writing pad. It is not enough that the librarian tells them all these in one period. He should keep a watch on them through the five years they are in the primary school. The teachers also should co-operate in instilling these habits in the children.

During their second visit, the period can be devoted to teaching them alphabetisation by improvising some word games, of which a few examples are given in the

Appendix. The little children will find the word games interesting as it would be a refreshing change from the routine of classroom teaching. So the word games may be taken up off and on when they come to the library during library periods until the librarian is convinced that the children have thoroughly understood alphabetical order. Units 4 to 11 can be taken up at the middle school stage that is, in upper primary classes when teachers would start giving the children assignments and projects that would necessitate research. The first four library periods of class six may be devoted to instructing them in Units 4 to 11 – one period for Units 4 to 7, two periods for Units 8 to 10 and one period for Unit 11.

When Units 4 to 7 are dealt with they should be shown the different parts of a book and explained how these could be useful during their research when they look for the material pertaining to the topic they are investigating. They must also be given some practical training by giving them some subject heads and asking them to find out the essay on the subject in any of the reference books. Presuming the school has a computer department and is teaching the children the use of computers the students must also be told about the vast possibilities of internet and given links to different search engines. If the library has computers, the librarian must give the students topics in different areas of knowledge as for example, history, science, and biography and ask them to go on the internet and collect information on those topics using appropriate search engines.

Units 12 must be taken up in the high school classes. They are not to be dealt with like the other Units. In the case of Unit 12, the librarian must organise a Literary Club that should meet once a month when the members would discuss a book. The membership should be limited to a maximum of ten children. The librarian must choose only those children who are interested in reading. At the beginning of the month the librarian or one of the members may choose a book, preferably any of the latest additions, for discussion. All members will read the book and at the end of the month, one member will read a paper on the reason why he likes the book or does not like it. It would be followed by a critical discussion on the paper presented on that day. The discussion in effect would be a critical analysis of the book. The criticism may be immature but it will help the students develop their critical faculties. Apart from that it will give publicity to the book and those children who are stuck with a particular type of book as for example mystery stories would come to know there are books of fiction more interesting than mystery stories. It may also help desultory readers find their moorings. A copy each of this paper must be put up on the library bulletin board and the school notice board.

Coming back to the principles of library ethics, the most difficult ethical problem is discipline in the library. This is not included in the list given above because this is not something that could be taught; this has to be instilled in the students. Needless to say, maintenance of discipline is far more difficult for the librarian than it is for a teacher. The tradition and the formal atmosphere of a classroom keep most children from breaking the limits of decorum and that considerably helps the teacher maintain discipline in the class. At the most, the teacher may have disciplinary problem with three or four children and that can be dealt with. Apart from that, the teacher can afford to be a strict disciplinarian. In the school library, on the other hand, the atmosphere is and has to be informal as the children are not constrained to sit in one place but can move around to browse and select the books they want to read or to consult reference books to clarify some points discussed in the class. This is a situation that possibly triggers indiscipline.

The librarian, however, should tactfully and sympathetically deal with any case of indiscipline on the part of the children who come to the library and create an impression that he is a friend to whom the children can look up to for help. In other words, he should ensure strict discipline in the library without being too stern. So the school librarian has to bear in mind that discipline in the library is not the regimentation of the soldiers or the formal discipline of the classrooms. He should also refrain from insisting on the musty silence of adult public libraries.

The school librarian has to realise that school library is different from any other type of libraries including the children's public library; it is basically a research centre. It is comparable to a workshop and so there is bound to be some noise. Besides, the children of school age bubble with enthusiasm and naturally when they see, for example, a beautiful picture in a book or magazine he/she would get excited and would like to discuss it with his friend. The school librarian as well as the children's public librarian have to accept that fact and instead of curbing that enthusiasm in the name of discipline, allow it but contain it; he should only make sure that such enthusiasm does not break the bounds of decorum. It may be necessary for the children to discus with one another when they are doing some project or assignment and so they may be allowed the liberty to talk in undertones.

It must be brought home to the children that the library is a place to carry out intellectual work on their own and each one should respect the rights of the others to do their work. This discipline is analogous to the discipline that vehicles observe on the road. The vehicles for example keep to the left of the road and that helps avoid collisions and free movement of all vehicles. In other words, those who drive the vehicles respect the rights and freedom of the other vehicle owners who use the road. This is self-discipline and that is what is expected of the users of the library generally and it is the duty of the librarian to instil that in the children.

When a child comes to work in the library, he or she is seldom alone; there are always other students also working in the library at the same time and this gives them social training. When a child uses the library along with several others, each working independent of one another they learn to respect the rights of others. This is not something that can be *taught* by the librarian or the teacher; this is what they will unconsciously imbibe when they work in the library along with several other pupils. They realise that they have to observe silence in order not to disturb their peers who they see are working in the library as they themselves are. They realise how they would be disturbed if someone else makes noise or disturbs the quiet of the library. However, there could be a few who do not understand this and in such cases, the librarian has to intervene and tell them the necessity of maintaining silence. Thus they learn to respect law and to live as responsible and law-abiding members of democratic society.

In a group of about fifty or more children, possibly there could be an *enfant terrible* or two. So such boys – and girls, less frequently though – can be expected to find in any school. They may have to be reprimanded when they behave in a manner that is not acceptable in the library and if that fails, they may be reported to the headmaster for necessary action. In spite of that, if they persist in their misbehaviour, those children may be referred to the school counsellor for counselling, in case the school has a counsellor, and if that too does not yield the desired result, the help of the parents concerned may have to be sought. Under any circumstance, such children should not be denied any of the library privileges as long as they are on the rolls of the school.

All that we discussed so far is about the tasks to be carried out during periods in the library. The library periods are intended to expose them to books hoping that it would create in them an interest in recreational reading. The co-operation of teachers is essential in drawing children's attention to good books. He must speak about books and fictional characters in all his lessons and try to finish his teaching about five to ten minutes before the period gives over. That time must be utilised to read out some interesting passage from some book. For example, he may refer to Dickens' *Oliver Twist*, and give a short introduction telling them about his birth and his mother's death soon after he was born, leaving him an orphan. His life in the workhouse, where the beadle Mr. Bumble gave the children who were there very little food and how Oliver Twist was mercilessly punished when he asked for more food. After giving this introduction, he should read out that portion, beginning with Oliver Twist's request, "Please sir, I want some more." The teacher can stop after reading out the portion describing how he was thrashed and apprenticed to an undertaker. If the teacher can do this in such a way that it touches a tender chord in the hearts of children, they will run to the library at the earliest opportunity to borrow the book.

In fact, teachers of any subject can make children interested in general reading. Mathematics teacher, for example, can spend a few minutes to talk about Srinivasa Ramanujan. And he can tell the children the story (though of doubtful authenticity) of how Ramanujan found the registration number 1729 of the car in which he was going with Professor Hardy interesting. That may make some children read the biography of Ramanujan. But before mentioning any book, the teacher should make sure that the book is available in the school library. If the teacher knows that the book he is referring to is not in the library, he may ask the children to request the librarian to procure a copy of it. And he too must put in a word to the librarian to buy that book, saying that he has already told the children about it and the book would not be gathering dust in the shelf.

There is an unmistakable paradigm shift in the functioning and use of libraries in our country today when India along with all other nations in the world are suddenly pushed into the information age by the revolution that has taken place in the sphere of electronic science. World Wide Web popularly known as WWW, Internet, Information Superhighways, Virtual Library, slowly but surely emerging Electronic Library and so on and so forth have become a reality. The school librarians would be failing in their duty if they do not acquaint the juvenile library users and equip them with the skill to take advantage of all these technological developments.

4

Outreach Programmes

Most school librarians have a notion that their activities do not extend beyond the school premises and are limited to providing support to the educational programmes of the school. No doubt, that is the primary duty of the school librarian. He should, however, bear in mind that the school is not an isolated island but a part of the community that nurtures it and to which the school has a duty other than teaching the children who come there. There are many children who have dropped out of schools at different stages of their schooling and adults who could not complete the school education for various reasons but are eager to join the open school. There are also many men, women and children who have been deprived of the privilege of school education and had not had the opportunity to master the skill of reading and writing. The school library has to collaborate with the public library and non-governmental organisations to help out all these marginalised sections of society.

There could be many children of economically backward families who will be compelled to take up jobs on leaving the school. The families of those children, who are compelled to discontinue studies, perhaps do not have the means even to have two square meals a day. Now that these children have completed their school education, their families happily look forward to them taking up a job and supplementing the meagre income on which they had been subsisting till then. So these children are duty bound to help their families, sacrificing their studies. They have to be informed of the various jobs that are available to those who have studied up to as well as completed the secondary school education. In other words, information has to be provided to those who have failed as well as passed in the secondary school leaving certificate examination about suitable jobs that they could apply for. At the same time, there would be many boys and girls who wish to prosecute their studies. They have to be helped to find the university that offers the courses they are interested in. Some may want to go abroad for further studies. They should be provided with the information required for getting admission in the university that they look forward to joining. In short, the problems of all these people are "what next?" and it is for the school librarian, in the absence of a counsellor, to help them look beyond their school education.

Hence, the most important of the various extension services that the school library should undertake is career guidance. The librarian is not a counsellor but in case the school has no counsellor, the librarian should take upon himself the task of career guidance, although he is not a qualified counsellor. Even if there is a school counsellor, the librarian has to provide background materials that give information on vocations available to failed and passed high school/higher secondary students to help whoever is counselling. And in the absence of a professional counsellor, as stated above, the librarian assumes the role of a career counsellor. The background materials include handbooks and brochures, pamphlets and prospectuses, magazines and newspaper clippings of advertisements and other publications that give details about various Indian and foreign universities. Apart from these, information on different trades is also necessary because those children who do not intend to go to universities would like to know what job opportunities they have in India and abroad and the qualifications required for those trades or professions.

Although some children do not intend to go for university courses, they would be interested in joining some vocational training courses conducted by industrial training institutes (ITI), catering schools, hotel management institutes, nurses training schools, Polytechnics and various others that require only Secondary School Leaving Certificate or Higher Secondary Certificate, pass or fail, depending on the course the child intends to pursue. The school library should, therefore, collect and keep prospectuses of all such institutes and update them every year. Besides, the library should keep up-to-date information regarding the duration of courses as well as the fee that is charged or the stipend given to candidates for each of these courses conducted by the several institutes in the town as well as in the state and other states that impart training to school children.

It is up to the librarian to bring all these information to the notice of the children of the secondary and higher secondary classes. If the library has computer with internet connection, the librarian should note down the links to the web sites of all vocational institutions and colleges that the children are likely to seek admission to, in the country. And he must also note down the web links to foreign universities, particularly of those in China, Australia, the UK and the US. Seldom do children from our country go to universities of countries other than those mentioned above for undergraduate studies.

Apart from these, the career guidance centre should also have particulars about the various competitive examinations being carried out by the State and Union Public Service commissions for the posts of clerks and other jobs that do not require a college degree or any other diploma but only a pass in the secondary or higher secondary school examination. So if the library subscribes to the state gazetteer it would be a great help to such of those children who do not want or cannot afford to go for higher education but prefer an office job. In addition to that, the librarian should put up on the bulletin board of the career centre, clippings from newspapers of advertisements calling for applications by the State and Union Public Service Commissions. These will draw the attention of children to those job openings and prompt them to refer to the gazetteer for further information on it.

Several of those children who take up clerical or some other jobs after the school, may be aspiring to study for a university degree privately by post or on-line. There are many universities in our country today that conduct Distance Education in various disciplines and the successful candidates are awarded degrees by the parent university. So handbooks and prospectuses of those institutes must be available in the guidance centre. Along with these, particulars regarding open universities too must be available for reference in the shelves of the centre. The children should be made to understand that these degrees are considered equivalent to the degrees taken by attending regular courses for the purpose of employment as well as promotion. In fact, taking a degree while employed has an advantage as the person gets experience and seniority in his profession while he enhances his educational qualification(s). That would give him an advantage over his colleagues who have no college education, when considering for promotions in the department or institution in which he works.

There is no gainsaying that few schools produce a hundred percent passes at Board Examinations and possibly, some of the failed students may prefer to make the second attempt through open school. But it is not advisable to speak to a student about it as it would give him or her, the impression that the school expects he/she would fail and that would only help the child lose self-confidence. But there is no use purchasing the prospectuses and keeping them under lock and key, for these are not proscribed documents; nor are they censored. On the other hand, these must inevitably be brought to the attention of the children but that has to be done without making it very obvious. So these must be displayed in open shelves in a prominent place so that no child misses noticing them.

During the course of introducing the children to the resources available in the guidance centre, the librarian may take it in his hand and tell the children jokingly that it would be of use only to those who fail at the Board examination and it is not meant for them because he does not expect any of them to fail. And to din it into them, he may ask, "Do you think any of you would fail?" In one voice they would say, "No Sir." The librarian must end by saying, "Good, that is what all of us, the teachers and your parents wish for and expect too. So I don't want to take this. Anyway, let us leave it on the shelf." He may then tell them briefly in a casual manner what open school is and how it would be helpful to those who fail in the Board examination or those who were not fortunate enough to have the opportunity to go to a school. And it must be left on the shelf in a place where the children would always see that. So those few children who happen to fail at the examination would recollect what the librarian said about the open school and would approach him for particulars regarding the open school.

There could be several children who are compelled to discontinue their studies not because they are not interested or poor in studies. They had to discontinue because, as mentioned above, of financial difficulties. Some of the children pass out with very high scores and may be brilliant, with IQs far above the average and if given good education would come up in life to the advantage of his family and country. It would be unfortunate if they are denied the opportunity to go for higher studies. The librarian should therefore collect all information regarding various scholarships and educational loans available for students who wish to prosecute their studies but do not have the wherewithal to meet the expenditure that university education would involve.

There are many scholarships and educational loans available today and a student does not have to depend on his or her family to finance their studies. All nationalised banks in India and a few private banks (which, of course fleece by charging very high interest) offer educational loans. Particulars about these loans from these banks may be collected and kept in the guidance centre so that the children can get the necessary information. All these information may be gathered from internet also. These loans are to be returned with interest after the student concerned gets a job. So banks do not usually give educational loans to a student who intends to pursue studies in arts and science colleges as the possibility of getting jobs after taking a bachelor's and even a master's degree in arts or sciences is remote. On the other hand, it is easy for a child who goes for professional courses to get these loans. The reason is obvious. The banks reasonably expect the latter to get a job soon after or even within a year of completion of his course so that he would be able to repay the loan. Similarly, there are many scholarships offered by various organisations (including caste based organisations) also and information about these too must be made available at the guidance centre. In the interest of children, the librarian may advise them to seek loans from nationalised banks rather than private banks.

Today, the tendency among children is to take up some professional courses like medicine, engineering, agriculture, veterinary science and such others. In fact, if they fail to get admitted to any of these courses the children look for admission in any arts and science colleges. Admissions to professional courses are not based on the marks they score in the qualifying examination only. The central and state governments conduct competitive examinations and admissions are given on the basis of the performance at those examinations. Some states take into consideration a certain percentage of the marks obtained by the candidate at the qualifying examination. But all states and the centre insist on securing a certain minimum marks in the qualifying examination for a candidate to appear for the competitive examination. The guidance centre, therefore, should necessarily have particulars about all competitive examinations held by the central government and different states as well as some private institutions, several of which conduct their own examinations.

It is desirable that the school librarian interacts with parents too in connection with career guidance because unlike in the US and European countries children in India usually go by the advice of their parents. So the librarian must utilise the Parent Teacher Association to find out what the parents have in their minds about their children's future. The advantage in using this forum is that most parents would be present at the meeting of this Association. Besides, the headmaster and all subject teachers including physical training and craft instructors would be at hand to give their opinions. A meeting of the Parent Teacher Association could be called a month or two after the school reopens specifically for the purpose of discussing children's career. Hence, the one-point agenda must be 'careers for children.' First of all, the librarian must acquaint the parents about the various openings in the employment market for those who have completed secondary and higher secondary courses. They must also be told about the universities to which their children could be sent and the different courses of study in those universities. After briefing about all that and inviting them to visit the career guidance centre in the library any time convenient to them, they must be asked to have one-on-one conference with teachers.

Let the parents and teachers interact. Teachers are the best judges of a child's abilities and aptitudes and they will be able to tell the parents authoritatively what course would be the most suited for a particular child. Based on the teachers' opinions and on their own aspirations for and observations of their children, the parents can discuss the issue with their children. Many a time the child may not be interested in the career his/her parents want him or her to choose. The Parent-Teacher Association meeting must be followed up by talks by professionals on different careers, to which not only the students but their parents too should be invited. One career meeting must be organised every month, if possible. Today, there are many openings for educated youth and it is not easy for the parents or the children to decide. Hopefully, after listening to career talks by professionals in the respective fields and taking into cognisance the views of the children, it should not be very difficult for parents and children too, to come to a decision.

Besides this, the librarian should have a conference with the parents of kindergarten children (in case the school has a kindergarten section) or/and lower primary school children in the course of the first term every year. The parents may be invited to the library. The librarian must take them round and show them the toys and books that are in the library and how much the children are making use of all those facilities that the library provides. No doubt, some parents would be shocked to find and disapprove of toys being in the library which people normally associate with books. But it may be explained to them how toys would help as a means to attract the children into the library and how children can be gradually guided to books.

At this conference, the necessity to restrict the time their children spend on computers or/and television must be brought home to the parents. The educated parents may be requested to insist on their children borrowing books form the library and to make sure they read those books. If, however, the children do not read for themselves the parents must find time to read out those books to their children. This is an opportunity for the librarian to discuss the reading interests of the child with the parent concerned and seek their co-operation in improving the child's reading taste. At the same time, the librarian would be able to know from the parents more about their child, like what his interests are, how he spends his time, how much time does he spend on studies and general reading and other personal traits. Those inputs will help the librarian guide the reading of the child.

In every school, possibly there would be on its rolls at least a few disabled children. The word disabled with reference to a child (or an adult) denotes a person who is by birth or later in his life deprived of his/her physical or/ and mental ability. Some physical and mental disabilities like retardation and problems with vision and hearing may not be evident or noticeable unless they are severe cases. These disabilities, whether severe or not, are a handicap for the children concerned. Hence it can be said that disabled children are naturally handicapped because they are at a disadvantage vis-á-vis children whose physical and mental faculties are not in any way impaired.

But all handicapped children may not be disabled. For example, children who are from economically backward and socially marginalised sections of society are not to be categorised as disabled. But they are handicapped. Governments both at the centre and of the states have recognised this fact in the case of socially depressed sections and they are given reservation. But children from families of economically backward section belonging to the so-called higher castes are denied reservation although they too are handicapped, which is palpable injustice.

Beatrice Wright defines disability as "a condition of impairment, physical or mental, having an objective aspect that can usually be described by a physician (while) handicap is the cumulative result of the obstacles which disability interposes between, the individual and his maximum functioning level." Typical of those of the privileged class, she seems to ignore the handicap caused by socio-economic factors when she defines the terms disability and handicap. Consciously or unconsciously, they tend to sideline socio-economic factors. In our country, there are thousands of children who are handicapped on account of caste and class into which they are born. A child born in a family of a caste that had been depressed and denied education for generations and a child born in an indigent family of whatever caste are handicapped. Almost all school drop-outs are from these sections. The extension services of the school library should reach out to all types of handicapped children, which we shall discuss presently.

The majority of the people of India, even among the educated class view the disabled as a sort of ill omen and their parents tend to neglect and often abuse such children. This is inhuman. It is estimated that there are not less than 60 million disabled (children and adults) in the country. A decade and a half back, the Government of India had passed the Persons with Disabilities (Equal Opportunities, Protection of Rights and Full Participation) Act, 1995, (PAD) bringing blindness, low vision, leprosy-cured, hearing impairment, locomotor disability, mental retardation and mental illness within the purview of this Act. And in 2007, India ratified UN Convention on Rights of Persons with Disabilities. However, the law, which is flawed and cries for amendments, is yet to be implemented, reflecting the callous attitude of the people of the country in general and the government in particular to the disabled. A discussion of the law and its implementation is beyond the scope of this book. What is intended to be stressed here is the attitude of the people of our country towards the disabled. At the same time, it has to be pointed out that children with disabilities are not to be pitied but treated as any normal child, giving them opportunities to develop their innate talents. That responsibility lies with the government.

The school librarian would not have to deal with children of all kinds of disabilities that are listed in the

PDA because severely disabled children are sent to special schools catering to specific disabilities. But the school librarian may have to deal with the disabled during literacy drive or counselling parents. Among school children also there could be some with myopia, low vision, hearing impairment, slight mental retardation, autism (a pervasive developmental disorder, often associated with mental retardation, communication disorders and abnormality in inter-personal relationship), dyslexia (a neurological ailment marked by the inability to read and bears no relation to the child's intelligence) and some such less noticeable disabilities. But there may be a few more visible ones like lameness due to accidents or poliomyletis, and other minor disabilities like hearing impairment. Lameness, of course, is very obvious but not slight hearing impairment, which however, is easy to find out. If a child does not turn back when called, the librarian may presume the child is hard of hearing.

The librarian or the library attendant has to help children who walk with crutches or are lame and find it difficult to take books from the shelves, in case he finds that they are unable to do it themselves. This must, however, be done without making it obvious. He should also refrain from asking children with disabilities personal questions even if he empathises with them. If he is so curious to know about it, he may casually ask the concerned child's parents or guardians when discussing the child with them. Even the temptation to do that must be resisted. However, if they voluntarily speak about it, listen to them and tell them that it is not a big impediment for the child to make use of the library. He can assure them that he is always there to help the child.

Many people have a tendency to talk condescendingly or in a condescending tone to a physically disadvantaged child. The librarian should talk to a disabled child as he would to any normal child. At the same time, there is no need to pretend not to have noticed the disability and he should not feel embarrassed to use words like "running" when speaking to a lame child; similarly do not hesitate to use words like "deaf" when talking to another child in the presence of one who has problem with hearing. These children are aware of their own problems. Other children may sometimes innocently mock them but if the librarian finds any such instance, it must be discouraged.

As far as possible, there should be no architectural barriers like steps at the entrance and at doors between rooms of the library. These must be avoided. And never house the school library in a duplex accommodation or one with a mezzanine floor. Apart from making it difficult for lame children, it is not easy for the librarian to maintain discipline when there is more than one storey because school libraries seldom have more than one librarian. Needless to say, one person cannot supervise two storeys simultaneously. That may help vandalism and create problems of discipline.

As mentioned above children with severe disabilities are not usually admitted in regular schools which have no facilities like specially trained teachers and necessary equipment to deal with their special needs and education. The government and some non-government organisations run special schools for them and they go to those schools. That there are not enough special schools in our country and some of them run by religious organisations are very expensive is a different matter. So the librarians of ordinary schools do not have to plan for providing resources for severely disabled children. But the school librarian has to be observant and if he notices any child with minor problems like visual and hearing impairment, dyslexia or autism he should report to the headmaster. The headmaster, in turn, must inform the parents concerned so that they can consult the specialist and get the child treated and provide the child with glasses or hearing aid as the case may be.

It may not be irrelevant here to point out two cases of severely disabled children studying in regular schools. One of them is Gayatri, a victim of osteoporosis, who had been confined to bed for three years. A brilliant student, she was in a regular government school in Thiruvananthapuram, Kerala. She passed the Secondary School Leaving Certificate examination with very high marks and had been enrolled in a leading higher secondary school. This was not an isolated case according to The Director of State Institute for Educational Management and Training (SIEMAT). Another is Arun Joy, a student of Assissi Higher Secondary School for the Deaf in Neerpara, Kerala. The Director of SIEMAT said, he "displayed a remarkable flair for tailoring, despite his handicap." The boy got over his speech and hearing impediments to enrol for a course in fashion technology. Incidentally, the words 'deaf' and 'blind' may be avoided in referring to those disabled children and instead use terms like 'hard of hearing' and 'visually impaired' respectively. In fact, even 'disabled' is considered inappropriate expression and they are referred to as 'differentially abled' because such children may have certain distinguishing or distinctive abilities.

Many parents give up hope when they detect any such defect in their child. The SIEMAT (Kerala) as well as the Directorate of Public Instruction and the Sarva Shiksha Abhiyan would conduct orientation courses for parents of those children on how to deal with children who are differentially abled. Generally, the society in our country still refuses to accept physically and mentally disabled children, thanks to some superstitious beliefs. When parents accept disabled children as such, it is their duty to create the right ambience for bringing out the latent talents of those children. In course of time, hopefully the attitude of the people will change.

Physically disabled children are in no way intellectually inferior to their able-bodied peers and in fact the IQs of several of them could be higher than the able-bodied. The physical disabilities do not affect their IQs adversely. However, it is generally believed that physical disabilities make a child intellectually superior. This too is a false notion. Such a notion has taken root by generalising the cases of a few physically challenged persons like Helen Keller and Stephen Hawking. The problem is that if children with severe disabilities like blindness are admitted in regular schools, let alone the absence of specially trained teachers, they will not be able to take advantage of the school library facilities. Libraries of regular schools would not have the funds to procure books in Braille, or electronic readers which are usually very expensive and the schools concerned cannot afford to spend so much for the sake of one or two children that may be admitted once in while. Apart from that, even if the libraries are equipped the librarians of regular schools are ignorant of the ways of dealing with such children.

It is, therefore, desirable that hearing impaired, visually impaired and mentally retarded children are admitted in special schools where there are specially trained teachers to handle those children. But those teachers are not trained in library and information science and to manage libraries of those schools, there should be specially trained librarians. In other words, librarians who are recruited for such schools must be given special in-service training to deal with children who have visual and hearing impairment. Hence, they have to learn Braille and sign language. The libraries of these schools would necessarily have books in Braille and on sign languages and other audio aids like radio, electromechanical transducers (electronic readers) for the blind and such other equipment. Unfortunately, in our country there are not enough schools to cater to the education of disabled children. Private agencies like certain religious groups and caste-based organisations in our country which today have entered the educational field are there with profit motive and may not be interested in running special schools. They do run a few special schools but the fees these schools charge are too high for most parents to afford and so special school for the differentially-abled, should be started by state governments or/and the central government. Children with minor disabilities like dyslexia, autism, stammering, colour blindness and other physical handicaps can be in regular schools.

Be that as it may, children who are handicapped socially and economically are likely to be retarded readers as they seldom get exposed to books before they are admitted to kindergartens/schools. Generally, social workers and even some educators erroneously believe that low IQs are the cause of their retardation and they conclude that children of socially depressed classes are naturally of low IQs. This, as pointed above, is a misconception. In fact, high, average and low IQs can be found both in the children of traditionally educated upper classes as well as in those of the marginalised classes. There is absolutely no evidence to claim that all children coming from families of the traditionally educated classes have high IQs and all those children of the parents belonging to the depressed classes have low IQs. It must be pointed out that such an erroneous notion is rooted in prejudice and not based on scientific evidence.

I had investigated and found that there was no correlation between general reading and IQ and my findings are given in my book, *Library Services for Children*. This investigation had led to the conclusion that IQ has no bearing on a child's general reading or to put it differently, general reading of a child is not dependent on his IQ. So it is wrong to think that all children of high IQs would naturally take to general reading of their own volition or be comparatively more interested in reading than those with average or low IQs. Retardation in reading, for example, is certainly not because of a child's low IQ but in most cases it is the effect of the environment in which the child has been brought up. To be specific, there is a relation between general reading and domestic background. It is not enough the parents are educated. Howsoever highly educated the parents may be, unless they take an active interest in their child's reading even a child with high IQ would not develop the reading habit. And a child with a low IQ is bound to develop the reading habit if the parents were to introduce him/her to the world of books at the impressionable age when the child is all the time at home. *Ergo*, it can be said that to a very great extent domestic background of the child is what makes a child a retarded or a gifted reader and domestic background is related to his family's social and economic status not to speak of the personal interest parents take in their child's education.

Nevertheless, children from the marginalised classes would be generally retarded on account of lack of pre-school training at home. This is but natural. It is because of the educational backwardness of their parents. Their parents may be literate but not educated or in many cases, even if they are educated, they may not have enough income to spend on picture books for their children. In many families of the middle class both parents may be employed and may have good income and their children may be attending good kindergarten schools. They have the money to buy books for their children but they do not realise the importance of providing children with books for general reading. They are happy if their children read the textbooks and do whatever homework the teacher gives. In fact, some parents positively discourage their children reading any book other than textbooks, for they consider general reading a waste of time. Even if some parents do realise and buy books for their children, they do not help the children read those books or find the time to read out stories from those books to their children.

Hence, for various reasons, most children would not have had the privilege of stories being read out to them during their pre-school period. So the school librarian has to pay special attention to the needs of these children. The library period in kindergarten schools and of lower primary classes may be devoted to story reading when the librarian may read out to children stories from books suitable for their age-group. Once they master the reading technique, he must pick up some one-act plays in which small children and/or animals are the characters and make the children act it out.

Apart from children belonging to the depressed classes, there could be several children from families of the privileged class who are retarded readers. Pre-school children of the privileged class may have all facilities and must have been provided with a large collection of expensive picture books at home. But unless parents take interest and ensure that the books they buy for their children are being made use of, those books will remain in the shelves gathering dust. Children of that age tend to play rather than read. If the parents do not make the child read or either the father or mother read out to the child stories from those books, howsoever intelligent a child is he would not develop an interest in reading.

The school authorities and the school librarian should realise that the school library is not an isolated island in the midst of the community which the school serves. They must understand the school and the school library owe their existence to the community around and is obliged to the community for its existence. It must be borne in mind that the community is the *raison d'etre* for the school in that locality and so it is not the members of the school alone that has a right to enjoy the resources of the library; the entire community which supports the school has the right. The Mudaliar Commission is justified when it suggests that the school library should be open to the public in places where there is no public library. I would suggest that the school library should be open to the public even in places where there is a public library as it can supplement the public library and vice versa. The school library, in that case, must be kept open outside school hours for the benefit of the public, for which the school librarian may be given an allowance by the local government, the corporation, the municipality or the panchayat as the case may be.

The Commission also suggests that during long summer vacations books suited to different age groups may be collected from various school libraries and kept in a centrally located building and the children encouraged to visiting this improvised library. The librarians of the schools from which the books are taken may in turn manage the library. This must be treated as over-time duty and the librarians on duty paid accordingly by the schools concerned. However, the co-operation of the parents is essential if this has to be successful because it is the responsibility of the parents to persuade their children to visit the library.

The obligation of the school library to the local community does not stop with keeping its doors open to the public. This would cast upon it the responsibility to serve the school dropouts and the illiterates. What can the school library do in the case of these two categories of people? There could be drop outs from the lower primary, upper primary and high schools, some of whom must have got employed under someone or some company while some others must be self-employed. There could be some who have failed to get any work and are idling away their time, swelling the ranks of the lumpen youth. Of course, most of those children may not be usually interested in reading but it is incumbent upon the public librarian to attract them to the public library, in which task the school librarian is obliged to help.

This is, in fact, one of the extension services of the school library also as much as it is of the public library. The public librarian may not know the parents or the residences of school drop-outs, which the school librarian is likely to be aware of. Moreover, the standard of most books available in the public library may be too high for those children and the choice would be very limited while there would be many books in the school library suited to their level of comprehension. However, their visits to the school library should be restricted to Saturdays and Sundays when the school is not in session. On the contrary, the public library should be open to them on all working days without any restriction whatsoever and the public librarian must pay as much attention to their needs as to that of other readers.

There is a section of our society comprising illiterates and neo-literates. No library, pubic or academic, can neglect this marginalised section of society. Every library has a duty to spread literacy or to put it differently, to eradicate illiteracy. The departments of social welfare and education of both state and central governments had initiated schemes with this objective in view but they have kept libraries out from this campaign without realising the importance of involving libraries. In fact, libraries should have been the mainstay of literacy campaign and public libraries should be in the forefront of government's literacy drive. The government officials concerned who planned the literacy campaign and the social workers seem to think that once a person learns to read, he would always be a literate. They do not understand that unless neo-literates are provided with books and encouraged to read, most of them would soon forget what they have learnt. The role of public libraries in precluding neo-literates from relapsing into illiteracy cannot, therefore, be ignored.

This applies to the school libraries also for the school library will be able to cater to them as much as the public library because the reading level of neo-literates would be the same as lower primary school children. But their reading interest may be different from that of the primary school children and the school librarian has to remember that fact when he selects books for the library. The teaching faculty of the school, as much as the librarian, should bear in mind that the school functions for the society in general and the neighbourhood community in particular. They cannot, therefore, shirk their responsibility and keep away from literacy drive. And it is for the school librarian as much as the public librarian to reach out to the neo-literates to prevent them from falling back into illiteracy.

A problem bigger than that of neo-literates and illiterates is that of retarded readers, some of whom could be those with low IQs, who may be found in all strata of society. This is usually congenital and such children have to be dealt with sympathy and tact. There are story books in English written in simple language with limited vocabulary for retarded readers of all ages, taking into cognisance the relation between the readers' age groups and interests. Unfortunately, I have not seen such publications in any of the Indian languages.

Another problem, which is rather not very common but cannot be ignored altogether, is kleptomania or in relation to the library, it may be called bibliokleptomania. Among a few hundreds of children occasionally one or two who suffer from this psychological malady could be found. This, as you know, is an irresistible urge or desire to steal something, which in this case is a book that usually may be what the 'culprit' does not need or is unable to use. So if diagnosed, it has to be dealt with sympathetically and the child has to be excused and treated by the school counsellor. As I said in my earlier book,[a] the bibliokleptomaniacs should not be taken to task if and when they are caught red-handed, for the principle of *mens rea* must be invoked in such cases and library rules regarding punishments given to pilferers should not be applied to them.

---

* The Multifaceted Librarian by V.M.Mohanraj, Ess Ess Publications, 2006, pp.16-17.

5

Resources

Resources are the life-blood of the school library as they are of any type of library and the value of a library depends not on the size or the architectural beauty of the building that houses the library or that of the collection but on the quality of the resources it has. Hence a mere collection of books, howsoever large it is, does not enhance the value of the library, be it school, college, university, special or public. On the other hand, the value of the library depends on the selection, howsoever small the collection may be. A select collection, in the context of the school library, means books suitable for the children of various age groups from the point of view of their contents vis-à-vis curricular and co-curricular needs, printing, illustrations and binding as well as those meant for recreational reading, both fiction and non-fiction. In addition, there should necessarily be books that meet the pedagogic and the educational demands of the faculty also, not to speak of the requirements of children with problems.

The resources include primarily the books and periodicals – in other words, the printed materials – which, apart from books and periodicals include clippings, maps, pictures and such other informational tools. The impact of modern technology on educational practices has further widened the horizons of school library with the result, it is now incumbent upon the school library to stock motion pictures, slides, sound recordings, audio/video cassettes, discs and other audio-visual aids. These necessitate film projectors, audio/video cassette and DVD players. In addition to these, today, there are many pieces of electronic equipment as for example the radio, television, and computer that have become as essential as books and periodicals in the school library.

There is no problem in purchasing electronic equipment like the radio, TV and computer for the library other than the availability of funds. However, it is only one-time allotment as there is no need to buy these more than once and there is no recurring expenditure on them except for some occasional minor repairs. In many cases, the librarian himself may be able to set it right. The criterion in the selection of any electronic equipment is the manufacturing company, which is known by the brand name and so there is no difficulty selecting them unlike in the case of books, which cannot be selected on the basis of the reputation of a publishing company. If the library is short of funds, it may purchase a computer and that can be used for playing DVDs, for then there will be no need to buy a separate DVD player. However, video/audio cassette players are inevitable but sooner rather than later these may become obsolete yielding place to DVD player, for DVDs are bound to replace cassettes, both video and audio. In fact, the cassettes and cassette players are already on their way out. So the only recurring expenditure will be for buying new educational DVDs. However, in selecting the cassettes and DVDs as much care as in selecting books should be taken. In other words, the selection of these electronic items has to be done on the basis of the same principles as the selection of books and periodicals.

That brings us to the problem of selection of printed and electronic materials of learning, which is the most important aspect of library administration. In earlier days when there were no electronic materials of learning, books and periodicals had been the only stock-in-trade of the school library. But now, electronic materials have become an inevitable part of the library collection and the selection of these is as difficult as, if not more difficult than, the selection of printed materials. Although electronic learning materials have an important place today, printed books still continue to be the most important resource material of the library. In selecting resources for the school library, the librarian has to bear in mind the most important principle of the philosophy of library services, which as Dr. Ranganathan puts it succinctly is, "Books are for use." The word *books* in the context of today should be taken to mean resources, which encompass both printed and electronic material. Above all, it implies that books for the library should not be selected indiscriminately without taking into consideration the interest of the clientele and the requirements of the community that the library serves.

However, it must be understood, tacitly supported by the publishing industry the e-book is nudging out its printed counterpart. It is difficult to foresee what its impact would be on the reading public in the long run. Time alone will show if it would replace the printed book altogether or only supplement the printed book. Some of the surveys conducted so far and the book market show that the reading public, particularly the younger generation tends to prefer e-books pointing to the possibility of disappearance of printed books in the not too distant future.

In Japan, it was reported, in the year 2002 approximately 25,000 titles were available on the e-book market and a thousand new titles are released on-line every month. It was found that on an average, 32,000 e-books were downloaded each month and the turn-out of the on-line publisher was to the tune of 300 million yen in the fiscal year 2002. A poll of 6,000 Internet users revealed that 9% had read e-books and 63% were interested in reading them. The e-book market, then, was about 0.04% of the printed book market, which amounted to 2.31 trillion yen in 2002 and the e-book market had been expanding at an annual rate of 40% to 60%. Almost a decade has passed since that survey was conducted and it may not be wrong to surmise, the demand for e-books had grown further during this period.

The Association of American publishers conducted a survey of the e-book market in 2001. They forecast that by 2005, e-books were expected to account for about 10% of the total consumer publishing market. The Electronic Publishing Forecast and Analysis, 2000-2004, in its report 'Digital Books and Print-on-Demand,' suggested that the U.S. market for digital books, including digital downloads and print-on-demand books will grow from 9 million US dollars this year to 414 million US dollars in 2004. Thus an incremental retail sales opportunity of 1.6 billion US dollars and total projected retail sales of 2.3 billion US dollars have been estimated, which expects the market for e-books to go up to an unprecedented 3.8 billion US dollars. It must be borne in mind that these figures do not even take into account the independent self-published author market in the US and represent the market of only the major publishing companies affiliated to the American Association of Publishers.

In 2002, at the Seybold Seminar in New York, it was

revealed that Microsoft Reader had an expected six million readers, which included four million Pocket PC e-book-enabled devices and two million downloads of Microsoft Reader for desktop or/and laptop computers. At the same seminar, Palm Digital Media, which was believed to be the largest e-book dealers, stated that it was catering to twenty million e-book readers and had 4,000 e-book titles that could be purchased through its web site, which had a hundred thousand customers and had a sale of 100 US dollars per customer. Adobe claimed they had more than three million e-book readers who downloaded not less than thirty million Acrobat e-books.

A survey conducted by Anderson Consulting in the US had come to the conclusion that the sale of e-book would be to the tune of 2.3 billion US dollars by 2005. No survey was conducted to verify if this prediction had proved correct. However, a more recent survey of e-book users conducted by Ingram Digital predicted the possibility of a surge in the adoption of digital textbooks. And it showed January-May sales in 2008 surpassed 2007 results by more than 400 percent. Ingram Digital's Education Solutions unit conducted the survey of a sample of its user base that exceeded 24,000 students and educators. "Data from the survey's 680 respondents revealed that when deciding whether to purchase a digital title, 47 percent believe that cost in relation to print copies is very important (and that naturally tilts them towards e-books). A similar proportion of respondents identified the convenience of e-books (46 percent) and interactive features (45 percent) as also being very important."

The Open e-Book Forum is an international non-profit trade and standards organization for the electronic publishing industry. Its annual report published at the close of 2003 states that during the period ending

September that year, the units sold have surpassed the one million mark for the first time in a single year. This, the Forum points out, shows an increase by 64% compared to the previous year. The sale proceeds from the third quarter alone, it was reported, went up 37% over that of 2002.

The statistics presented by the retailers corroborate what the Open e-Book Forum has stated. According to that, 1,038,086 units were sold during the first three quarters of the year 2003, which was an increase of 64% over the same period in the previous year when only 229,990 units were sold. They claim that 377,095 e-books were sold in the third quarter of 2003 alone. This fetched a sum of 2,591,469 dollars in 2003 and this was an increase of 37% over the same period in 2002, during which period they could sell for 1,893,437 dollars only.

The number of e-books published between January and September of 2003, was 2159, an increase of 74% while during the same period in 2002, only 1241 titles were brought out. The Open e-Book Forum reported in September 2003 that school children prefer to read books in digital form rather than in the printed form and naturally there had been an explosion of demand for e-books, particularly those of fiction in 2003. Researches in the US have revealed that the most popular categories of e-books are romance novels, science fiction and textbooks particularly of university classes. The college students can load all their textbooks for a semester into the reading device, as for example the one known by its trade name "Kindle," of Amazon.com, making it easy to carry around. The affluent businessmen who frequently travel around prefer e-books because a few hundred full-length e-books can be loaded into a pocket PC, which also holds their appointments and other information that they need. And it serves as a notebook too.

The problem with digitised books is its lack of durability. The *Doomesday Book*, a document compiled by William the Conqueror in 1085 has been preserved in an environmentally controlled facility and is still in a readable condition. On the other hand, its digitised version produced in 1986 lasted just twenty years because over time the magnetic patterns embedded in the computer disc degraded. However, scientists claim that they are now on the verge of finding a method to preserve digitised documents for millions of years from now. They found that "microscopic iron crystals moving within carbon nanotubes could hold computer data permanently. A team of physicists and materials scientists describes a technique of placing a single iron crystal only a few billionths of a meter wide inside a hollow carbon nanotube. Like diamonds, nanotubes are among the most stable structures in existence. Once inserted into the tubes, the iron nanocrystals act as data bits, physically sliding from one end of the tube to the other in response to an electric current and in the process registering either a "1" or a "0" in the binary language of computers."§

The advent of the electronic book, which is generally known as e-book, poses a problem as far as librarians in our country are concerned. Several librarians today are of the opinion that libraries in the future should be a place for digitised information rather than books, just because many of the developed countries are transforming libraries into total digitisation. But when India can have fully digitised libraries is a difficult question to answer because for the present it is unrealistic for India to digitise libraries, for which the readers are not prepared. No survey of the reading public of India has been taken to find out what they

---

* Derardelli, Phil, A Billion-Year Hard Drive, *ScienceNow Daily News*, May 29, 2009. (On-line)

want and so we are in the dark as to what the readers think of the future of libraries. Whatever it is, most libraries today are not computerised and majority of the people are not familiar with computers. Even in developed countries where computers are used by elementary school children, digitisation of libraries has not made much headway so far.

I surmise if a survey is taken in our country to find out people's attitude towards digitisation of libraries, the opinion of the reading public would be basically on the lines of economic classes. The library going people of the upper middle class who are computer savvy and who have computers at home may favour libraries to be places of digitised information while those who belong to the lower middle class and the working class, many of whom have no time to visit a library or the wherewithal to buy a computer do not care what the library has. And even those who visit libraries would prefer printed books for they are not familiar with computers and e-books.

But this attitude is bound to change because schools in most States in our country have introduced computer training and this will help attain a hundred percent computer literacy among the school children of today. It is heartening that even in rural areas children are being taught the use of computers in schools. Some children in towns and cities attend computer classes conducted by various private institutes and franchisees of computer dealers. However, although children have learnt to use a computer, they cannot afford to possess a computer today and after they leave school they may possibly relapse into 'computer illiteracy'.

However, with the pace of revolutionary changes taking place today in the field of electronics, it may not be too unrealistic to hope that the day is not far off when less expensive computers would be produced that are within the purchasing power of the common man. The possibility of laptops being used by children of all social classes as they use exercise books today should not be dismissed as pipe dream. It is not unrealistic to say that exercise books of today will have the fate of slates of yesteryears and that will pave the way for the wide-spread use of e-books.

Hence, as it stands today, there is no possibility of the e-book replacing the printed book completely in the immediate future. And it is difficult to foresee if the young readers of India who are accustomed to reading printed books from an early age today, would reject them altogether in favour of e-books. Possibly, they will, because by the time they grow up or at least by the time the next generation of children grows up, e-books will have replaced printed ones in all Indian languages too and all types of libraries in our country will have turned into digitised libraries.

Are the days of printed book numbered? I would say 'yes' and 'no.' Even if e-books begin to be preferred by the reading public, it can be said with certainty that it may take several, if not many, years to digitise all the books that had been printed till to date and those that are still pouring out of the press everyday all over the world as well as those that are presently out of print. The Copyright Act or the Intellectual Property Rights Act is another insurmountable impediment in digitising printed books that are in circulation today. It can, therefore, be expected that for many years to come printed books would continue to be in circulation side by side with e-books. Whatever is the prognosis, the librarian of today must set apart shelves for digital information sources and one day e-books are bound to push out printed books completely.

It must be borne in mind that the printed book appeared for the first time in 868 CE in China. The first printed book extant today is said to be one titled, *Diamond Sutra*, which is the most popular among the body of sutras and commentaries called *Prajnaparamita* that expounds the essence of the Mahayana Buddhism. In 1401, the Chinese invented movable clay type that made printing easier but mass production of printed books was made possible after the invention of printing press with replaceable/moveable wooden or metal fonts by Johannes Gutenberg between 1436 and 1440 only. The longer durability of the metal or wooden fonts compared to that of movable types helped continuous printing of a large number of books at a time.

A giant step forward was taken more than four centuries later, in 1886, in the process of printing with the invention of the linotype composing by Ottoman Mergenthaler. Further advance in the process was made when F. E. Gannett and W. W. Morey in collaboration with Morkrum-Kleinschmidt Company, Chicago developed teletype printing. This came into vogue in 1928 after Morey demonstrated the typesetter for the first time. Another major development in the history of printing process was the discovery of phototypesetting, which was done by using a strobe light and a series of optics to project characters from a spinning disc on to a photographic paper. The advent of computer, however, supplanted the phototypesetting process, thanks to the desktop publishing software that uses the same process for printing.

So we find, although printing of books commenced in the 9th century, it was confined to China and the technique did not permit the production of books on a mass scale. It was only after Gutenberg's discovery in the mid-fifteenth century that books began to be produced in large numbers in all countries and subsequent improvements in the printing processes gave a tremendous boost to the production of books. After the Renaissance, innumerable books began to pour out of the presses in the world every day. The total number of books printed over a period of six to seven centuries all over the world in various languages is, thus, unimaginable. If we were to arrange all those books in a single pile, it may perhaps extend hundreds of thousands of kilometres into space, far beyond the sun. Taking into account only classics as well as modern books of literary value and those informational books that have stood the test of time and would be of use to researchers, the number would be too much to be digitised in a decade or two with the present rate of conversion to digital form

As a result of the above mentioned developments in the printing technology, thousands of books and periodicals in nearly as many languages are now coming out of the press all over the world in a day. So for a long time to come, even if the task of digitisation of books is carried out day in and day out without break, it is doubtful if all the books published so far can be digitised within a decade. When that happens, the form of the library will not be what it is today. Perhaps, there may not be an institution like the library as we know it today and anyone sitting at home would be able to access any book he or she wants through the computer. Anyway, it is difficult to surmise what form the library would take in the future when e-books replace the printed ones completely.

Whether it is printed books or e-books that constitute the library, selection of books for the school library remains an important and difficult part of the duties of the school librarian. As a general principle, the librarian must guard against his personal interests and prejudices influencing his selection. The criteria should be the age group of the clientele and the educational activities of the school which comprise the curricular and co-curricular activities. In addition to his own selections, the librarian should get suggestions of teachers of the various sections and departments and prepare a consolidated list.

For the purpose of book selection, the students of these five sections – kindergarten (lower and upper), lower primary (classes one to five), upper primary (classes six to eight), secondary (classes nine and ten), higher secondary (classes eleven and twelve) – could be divided into four groups on the basis of their reading interests, tastes and vocabulary. The children of the kindergarten form one group, lower primary section another group, those of the upper primary classes the third group and the others, the secondary and the higher secondary students, constitute the fourth group. These, of course, are not watertight compartments, for they do overlap to some extent. For example the reading interest, taste and vocabulary of an average pupil of class five which is the final year of lower primary section may not be different from those of an average student of class six, the first year of upper primary section.

The selection of resources, whether it is printed material or electronic, demands the pooling of the expertise of the entire faculty and if need be, even of authorities in the subjects concerned beyond the school precincts. The school librarian can also seek, for example, the help of the staff of the local college and the librarians of public libraries in the town. He should collect and distribute flyers, publishers' catalogues and other book guides among the staff, teaching and non-teaching, in order to enable them to suggest books for the library keeping in mind the curricular requirements. Most teachers tend to select books in their disciplines that are strictly within the range of comprehension of school children but it is better that the school library has a few resource books of college level too to cater to the gifted children. In fact, at times, even the teacher himself/herself may have to refer to college level resource books to clear the doubts raised by some gifted students.

I have seen from experience that gifted children do take advantage of – and many a time teachers too find the necessity to refer to – books of university level, especially when problems related to certain recent developments are discussed in the class. Sometimes even encyclopaedias do not help as annual supplements are also received by the time they are outdated by at least one year. Of course, these days up to date information on any subject can be had on the Internet but still some recent publications on the subject will be helpful. So the teachers should be made to understand that it is desirable for the school library to have on its shelves, books that are a little above the standard of the school children.

The core collection in a school library, irrespective of the number of students in the school, should not be less than a thousand volumes, which includes certain essential reference books like encyclopaedias and dictionaries, gazetteers and year-books. The London County Council recommends 8 to 10 volumes per child – that is, in a school with an enrolment of 750 children the library should have 6,000 to 7,500 volumes on its shelves. These include reference books also. As far as the other books are concerned, needless to say, there has to be more books of fiction than those of non-fiction as it should be in any academic and public library.

Based on the form, the books may be broadly classified into two groups – reference books and books designed for consecutive reading. The former group comprises encyclopaedias, dictionaries, atlases, gazetteers, handbooks and such other fact-finding books. In the absence of reference books, the school library, which is primarily a reading centre, cannot serve as an information centre that it virtually is. In other words, it is so to say a resource centre to which children go to research. In selecting reference books for the library, care should be taken to select those that are suitable for the age group for which they are procured. It would be preposterous to acquire the Old English Dictionary, which is a multiple volume historical dictionary for the school library or a two-volume World Book Dictionary for the primary section if it has a separate sectional library. There are many dictionaries of English and Indian languages that are suited to the school students. In the case of encyclopaedias, a complete set of the Encyclopaedia Britannica, either in printed book form or in e-book form (DVD), may be procured for the secondary/higher secondary school library. But for the upper primary students Britannica Junior Encyclopaedia is the ideal one. There is also Oxford Junior Encyclopaedia and all these are available on-line.

Most importantly, the school library should have a larger number of fiction books than non-fiction. The ratio of fiction to non-fiction books varies in relation to the age groups – the lower the age group the more the number of fiction than non-fiction. So the children of lower and upper primary classes should be provided with a larger number of fiction books than informational books and the ideal ratio of fiction to non-fiction in preschool would be 5:1 and for primary schools, 4:1. The ratio of fiction to non-fiction in middle schools should be 3:1 while the ratio of fiction to non-fiction books for the students of secondary and higher secondary classes should be 3:2. The librarian should specially ensure that the books for the pre-school and primary school children are beautifully and some of them fully illustrated. The pre-school library should have many "talking" books and a few such books must find a place in the library of the lower primary school also. We have dealt with the categories of books that should necessarily be in the school library are given below:

1. Reference books.
2. Juvenile fiction. The school library must have a separate section for this category.
3. Informational books. These are basically non-fiction books, aimed at enhancing children's knowledge. These are books of various branches of science, history, language, geography, civics and such other books.
4. Classics in literature. These include book of fiction and drama as well a belles-lettres which is primarily books of poetry and literary essays in the regional language of the state in which the school is situated as well as in English. Translations of fiction books in English and in the regional languages. The primary school library may have abridged versions of classics in fiction.
5. Non-fiction books written in popular style for children, intended for light, recreational reading.
6. Books for retarded readers – both fiction and non-fiction. There are many juvenile books in English that are written specially for retarded children. In regional languages too a large number of children's books are available that are suitable to retarded readers.
7. Books for neo-literates.
8. Books that supplement curriculum. These are not exactly textbooks but those that are tailored to meet the requirements of curriculum.

9. Copies of textbooks of various subjects other than those used in the school must be kept in a separate shelf and made available not only to the staff but also to those children who ask for any of these.
10. For the faculty: Pedagogical and Psychology books. Methodology, behavioural science and others which are useful for teachers.
11. Tools of the library: These include publishers' lists and books on library science, as for example classification and cataloguing – particularly, books on school library.
12. In addition to these, the school library should have newspapers, magazines, pamphlets, clippings, pictures, photographs, maps and charts.

N.B. Care should be taken to buy books, cassettes, CDs and DVDs that are appropriate to the age group of children of each of the different sections of the school.

The first step in book selection is budgeting. Some books on school libraries published in the US deal with this aspect of a school librarian's work elaborately like budgeting for a huge establishment. Such business practices may be applicable to big libraries as for example, the National Depository Libraries or university libraries. But budgeting in school libraries is a simple matter. When the annual allotment for the library is known, the school librarian should go by the rule of thumb. First of all set apart the required amount for replacing the lost or damaged books – not all but only those that have been in great demand and the librarian thinks, have to be replaced necessarily. The rest of the amount may be distributed for the purchase of fiction and non-fiction books for recreational reading in the ratio stated above and source books of different disciplines on the basis of the lacunae that have been observed in the course of the previous academic year. The bulk of the allotment may be kept for the purchase of new books that would be hitting book stores in the course of the current year.

The new books must be selected taking into consideration to the extent possible, the demands of the children and the staff. As far as the children are concerned, a certain amount should be allocated for each age group. If, however, it is only a single unit school, as for example elementary, middle, high and higher secondary, this differentiation is not necessary. In the case of a comprehensive school comprising all sections, lower and upper primary as well as secondary and higher secondary classes, it is imperative that each section is provided for in the budget. Needless to say, the allotment should be higher for the secondary and higher secondary sections because the books meant for them would be more expensive than those for the lower and upper primary classes.

When a new book is received in the library, first of all it has to be collated and if everything is in order, the librarian should examine the quality of the format critically. He must first verify if the binding is attractive and strong enough to withstand the rough handling by the children. The colour of the paper used for the book is very important and the librarian cannot overlook it. The paper should be of light cream colour and smooth but without being shiny. The print should be bright and clear and the font, suited to the age group for which the book is meant. Most importantly, the book should be well-illustrated and in the case of books for the lower age groups; the more colourful the pictures are, the better. Most of the children's books that are put in the market by reputed publishers would satisfy these conditions.

In certain cases, especially in the case of juvenile books in Indian languages, the librarian may use his discretion and relax these conditions because not many books for children come out in Indian languages. Of those that are in the market, few satisfy the conditions stated above regarding the get up. If these conditions are to be met, the cost of production would go up and the price will be too high not only for a majority of the people but also for school libraries to purchase. The funds for school libraries are usually too meagre to buy many expensive books and large number of copies of the book may remain unsold and that precludes the publication of expensive books in Indian languages. Thus, school libraries have no choice but to buy whatever is available or not to buy at all leaving them with an inadequate collection of books in the genre of juvenile literature in regional languages. So if the books are acceptable from the point of view of contents, the librarian has no choice but to overlook the format.

Books, traditional audio-visual aids and electronic equipment like the television and computer are not the only resources that a school library should have. In the library attached to a kindergarten or primary school or a composite school which has both or any one of these sections, a huge collection of well-selected picture books and simple story books is not enough. The library of these schools should necessarily provide toys too which, for these libraries, are as important as books and electronic equipment. Toys may include not only moving ones like cars and trucks but also dolls and jigsaw puzzles. These must be strong but do not pose any danger of injury. Apart from these, board games, building blocks and word games like the Scramble, Lexicon and Word Building may be procured. In fact, there are myriad such games in the market today. In the early stages before children fully master the mechanics of reading and take to reading books on their own, these would keep the little kids interested in the library. These tiny tots who come to the school are attracted by these and not by books and they would look upon the library as a place to enjoy. Creating such a mindset would be the first step that could be the launching pad for taking the children to the world of books.

The inexorable and inevitable changes taking place in the world of libraries fuelled by the electronic revolution is bound to engulf our country sooner or later and digitised libraries would replace the present libraries in schools. However, it is too optimistic to think that such a situation will arise in the near future and if at all it does, it may take several decades for India – why, it may take decades even for the developed countries to write the obituary of the traditional school library. When it happens, instead of books, the school library will have as many computers on its tables as the number of readers expected to use the library at one time.

When a child enters the school library for the first time, there would be nothing to attract him and create in him an urge for reading. Instead of the colourful covers of rows and rows of books stacked in beautifully polished wooden or steel shelves, his eyes will be met by drab computers that sit uninvitingly on the tables. And he will not get the feel or the smell of books. It is difficult to foresee how the school children would react then.

6

Resource Persons

The interface between the resources and the clientele of the school is the resource person(s) and the chief resource person of the school library is the librarian, if there is only one professional personnel and it is the chief librarian as well as the assistant librarian(s) in case there are more than one professional librarians. It is the interface that finds the material or information for the reader and brings the relevant material or information to the notice of the concerned reader. The interface puts into practice two important principles of the philosophy of library service which, in the words of Dr. Ranganathan, are 'every reader his book' and 'every book its reader.'

It is, therefore, essential that the educational authorities and administrators, not to speak of the headmasters of schools, realise that the most important factor in the school library is the librarian. But the educational authorities in our country are yet to understand the necessity for professional librarians in schools. A library without a professional librarian is like a hospital without a qualified medical officer. As pointed out in the earlier chapters, few schools in our country have adequate libraries but even some of those schools that have fairly good libraries do not have professional librarians! As a result, in spite of having good libraries, library service in these schools suffers. If there is no good library and a librarian in the school, it is incumbent upon the headmaster to pressure the authorities, the education department or the management as the case may be, to appoint a professional librarian and organise a library in the school of which he is at the helm. That the successful implementation of the educational and social objectives of the school library depends primarily on the librarian cannot be denied.

Taking for granted that necessary resource material and other equipment are available, the library cannot achieve these aims which are co-extensive with the school that the library subserves without a professional librarian. So every school should have a fulltime, professionally qualified librarian who is accountable only to the head of the institution and has the unfettered academic freedom to organize the library as well as to carry out the library programmes. It is up to him to guide and stimulate the clientele which comprises the students as well as the members of the various faculties. Needless to say, the success of the library depends to a large extent on the co-operation of the teachers.

The term 'professional librarian' denotes a librarian who is a college graduate in any discipline holding, in addition, the credentials of a librarian. In other words, his minimum qualification shall be a bachelor's degree in humanities, sciences, law, engineering, medicine or any subject as well as a bachelor's degree in library and information science. However, to be successful school librarians it is preferable for graduates in library and information science to undergo special training that they do not have at present. In fact, the Union Ministry of Education was seized of the problem and in 1962 the Directorate of Extension Programmes for Secondary Education (DEPSE) sponsored an All-India seminar on school libraries at Bangaluru (Bangalore) under the direction of the doyen of librarians Dr. S.R.Ranganathan. This Seminar had made many recommendations aimed at improving school library service. The most important of these recommendations was about the training of school librarians.

In order to facilitate the implementation of these recommendations the DEPSE constituted a Working Group, which was entrusted with the task of drafting a suitable syllabus for the purpose. The Working Group met in Vadodara (Baroda) in 1964 and drafted a syllabus with an educational thrust. A programme for the training of school librarians was also chalked out at that meeting. The next year an orientation course for the prospective directors of the training programme was conducted in Allahabad and Bangaluru (Bangalore). After this the Union Ministry of Education drew up a scheme for a short training course – an in-service training course – for school librarians all over the country. The State governments, which were urged to take necessary action to carry out this training programme, did not follow it up, maybe because there were no proper school libraries and qualified librarians in any of the states! And we were back to square one.

The school librarian, unlike the librarians of other types of libraries, should know the reading interests and tastes, hobbies, academic attainments and behavioural peculiarities of every child in the school. In fact, he should know the educands as much as the tools – books, periodicals, clippings, films, audio and video cassettes, DVDs, computers and such other stock-in-trade of the library – that he handles. It is, therefore, imperative that apart from being proficient in library technique, he must have a good grounding in child psychology. He must also be conversant with the pattern and content of education in the country and particularly the syllabus of the Examination Board to which the school is affiliated. In our country there is more than one Examination Boards. Each state government has its own Board of examination and so has the central government which is the Central Board of Secondary Education (CBSE). Apart from these, there are non-government Boards also as for example, the ICSE, ISC and IB (International Baccalaureat). The government schools and aided schools in each state have no choice and are necessarily affiliated to the Boards of the State Governments concerned. All Sainik Schools and Navodaya Vidyalayas, Public Schools (These are non-denominational residential schools affiliated to the Indian Public School Conference and run on the lines of British Public Schools, like Eton and Harrow. Ironically, although known as Public Schools, these are *private* schools) and private schools have opted for either the CBSE or the ICSE/ISC Board while International Schools and a few private schools have chosen to affiliate themselves to the IB Board.

Many educationalists, therefore, are of the view that in addition to an intensive training in librarianship, a school librarian must have basic courses in education with, desirably, teaching experience. Some of them stress the latter and expect the school librarian to be a well-qualified pedagogue. So, they opine, besides the requisite courses in education, those who aspire to be school librarians should cover an extensive curriculum in library science. In either case, it has been generally accepted that the school librarian should qualify in two professional fields. The school librarian would, thus, be as much an educator as he is an expert in library science. But a school librarian, whether he has undergone a course in pedagogy or not, is more an educator than a librarian; hence he has to pay more attention to the educational functions than to technical matters. With the advent of computers in libraries, Information Science also has been included in the syllabus for courses in librarianship and this, no doubt, is a necessary addition today.

Until recent times, in our country, school librarianship was looked upon as a profession that does not call for any specialized training. Most people, even among the educated class, were under the impression, that any literate could be a school librarian and it was considered disgraceful for a degree holder to be a librarian, particularly school librarian. This attitude towards the profession persisted even in the 1950s! But those days are gone and the educationalists as well as the people in general have begun to recognise librarianship as a dignified profession and the librarian as a professional who has to be qualified in librarianship. The educationalists, educational administrators and the educators seem to have accepted the fact that even the school librarian has to be at least a college graduate who is required to have been trained in the field of librarianship just as a teacher or a doctor is expected to, in the relevant professional field. A librarian without the professional qualification is in no way different from a quack.

However, the educators still do not consider the school or college librarian a member of the teaching staff. In their eyes only a pedagogue is a teacher and because the librarian does not use a black board and chalk or his voice in teaching the children, he is not regarded as a teacher. It is not generally understood that the school librarian helps the children learn not just one subject or two as most teachers do but all subjects that are in the curriculum. The children usually run up to the library and ask the librarian whenever they are not able to get a doubt cleared in the class. A good school librarian seldom fails them. He finds a book that helps them get their doubts cleared and many a time explains to them what they do not understand. And he also helps members of the teaching staff find material on topics that occasionally come up for discussion in the class and are not in the prescribed textbooks. Yet he is looked upon as a non-academic professional and this outdated view is taken advantage of by some private schools to deny them the scale of pay equivalent to that of the teachers. All these private school managements do so for economic reasons. But not so in the case of Sainik Schools, which too do not treat the librarian on a par with teachers. This could be because Sainik Schools are under the Defence Ministry and defence officers in charge of these schools are not educationists

In this information age, the school librarian is more than an educator. He is, as the librarians of all other types of libraries are today, an information navigator also. Nevertheless, until the entire student population of schools in India is ready to accept digitisation of libraries, it is better school libraries adopt a via media position and have 'hybrid libraries' catering to both classes of children, computer literates and computer illiterates. Similarly, public libraries too should have both printed and digitised books so that no section of literates is deprived of the use of the public library. However, librarians of school libraries, as in the case of public librarians, apart from being navigators for the information superhighway, should also take the role of trainers during this interim period. As navigators they are expected to help readers access whatever book they want to read and help researchers find information related to the topic they are researching on the internet. As trainers, therefore, they are not expected to teach computer engineering but should help the clientele learn about using computers to access e-books and retrieve information with the help of search engines.

Computer coaching classes are all in the private sector and the fees that they charge are exorbitantly high with the result most of those who want to learn the use of computers are not able to. So a course in computer use must form a part of school curriculum in our country and should be made a compulsory subject in schools. The objective is to achieve a hundred percent computer literacy. This is achievable if the new Constitutional amendment making education a fundamental right is sincerely implemented. In our country, the school librarians who, as pointed out in chapter 4, Outreach Programmes, are expected to be in the forefront of literacy drive along with public librarians, should shoulder this responsibility to some extent and this can be done during the normal working hours of the library when the students come to the library to read and/or research. In fact, the school librarians are favourably placed to supplement by helping the children practise what they learn in their computer classes.

A survey conducted in the US found that 85% of Americans think it is important for libraries "to provide computers and on-line services to children and adults who do not have their own computers." It may not be wrong to say, that in our country not less than 90% of school children may not be having computers at home and would certainly be glad to make use of the services of the computer teachers and school librarians in their schools as well as public librarians to master the use of computers for gathering information on the internet. Needless to say, school librarians' role as computer trainers is confined to familiarising the children with various search engines and teaching them to retrieve through those search engines whatever information they are looking for.

Today, in the UK and the US, mere degree, even post-graduate degree in library science, is not enough to be children's librarians, which all school librarians are. In other words, children's librarian in these countries specialises in working with children. So the librarians who work with children in public libraries and school libraries are expected to have undergone specialised training for working in school libraries or/and children's public libraries.

Children's librarians, be it of school libraries or public libraries, in the UK for example, are expected to have undergone specialisation after they qualify themselves in librarianship and have had experience in library work in general, preferably in an adult public library. First of all, a school librarian or a children's librarian in a public library will have to deal with adults also and secondly, the school library being the foundation on which the entire edifice of the library movement stands, is the cradle of adult public library users. It is here library awareness is created and the clientele of all types of libraries, especially public libraries, is generated.

The Library Association in Britain holds an examination in library work with young people. This is conducted as an alternative part of the final examination taken by those who have passed the Registration Examination. A pass in this qualifies the successful candidate, after a minimum of three years experience in an approved library, for entry on the roll of Chartered Librarians as an Associate of the Library Association. The final examination demands a wide knowledge of books published in various disciplines, reference works and juvenile books suitable for different age groups as well as for backward readers. The candidate should also have knowledge of bibliographies and other guides for book selection. Apart from child and adolescent psychology, he should know their linguistic and reading ability. He is also required to be conversant with the planning, equipment, organisation, methods and objectives as well as with the curricular and co-curricular needs of schools and school libraries. Finally, he is expected to know the possibilities of co-operation between schools and public libraries. Apart from lectures, visits and discussions, covering the syllabus of the Library Association examination, practical instruction in voice production and story telling is imparted.

In the US, each State has its own rules and regulations regarding qualifications for school librarians. Several States, however, insist on school librarians holding certificates issued by the Department of Education of the State concerned. In addition to the prescribed course in library science, this involves twelve to twenty-four credit hours in education. This implies that the school librarian is not just a librarian; he is both a librarian and an educator. Hence, in the US, it is expected that in addition to the professional qualification of the individual, the aspiring full-time school librarian should have had teaching experience or undergone courses in pedagogy. Alternatively, a qualified teacher with a degree in education who had had training in library science could also be a full-time school librarian. In addition to the minimum qualifications stipulated by the State, local requirements, like passing a special examination in library science, too has to be met. Interestingly, the Graduate

School of Library and Information Science of the University of California is conducting specialized in-service training courses in management for selected senior librarians.

In our country, teaching experience is not considered a necessity for school librarians; nor is specialisation in the field of children's librarianship. However, the school librarian should have a Bachelor's or Master's degree from a recognized university in the country or abroad in any discipline followed by a Bachelor's or Master's degree in library and information science. This is the minimum qualification required for a person who intends to be a librarian in any type of library and the school librarian is not required to have undergone any specialized training. This drawback can be overcome if the syllabus includes a paper on child and adolescent psychology and another on organisation, methods and objectives of the educational system in India. If that is done by all universities, a separate course for specialising in children's library work may not be necessary.

But the future role of the librarian and the very profession of librarianship remains a question mark. When e-books and e-journals supplant printed books and journals and digital libraries replace the traditional libraries, the school librarian would neither be an educator nor a person who need to know library techniques; he should be an information navigator. As pointed out earlier, it may take many years for the digitisation of all printed books.

Educational and professional qualifications apart, the most important qualification that a librarian should possess is his personality, which is the sum total of his physical and intellectual traits. He has to be mentally alert, enthusiastic, friendly and co-operative and above all he should have a pride in his profession. It is imperative the school librarian is a compulsive reader and must have a wide knowledge of the world of books. If only he has all these qualities, would he be able to create the right ambiance – a homely and scholarly atmosphere – in the library. That would go a long way in attracting children into the library and making the time they spend in the library a pleasurable and edifying experience. But it must be understood that the age group which he is dealing with can be extremely demanding and annoying. So the school librarian (also the librarian of a children's public library) has to be patient and should not get flustered losing his equanimity and temper even in the most trying situations. This, doubtless, is a tall order but he must try to keep his cool always.

The Secondary Education Commission of 1953 recommends that the school librarian and professional assistants, if any, are to be treated as members of the teaching faculty.* The chief librarian, the Commission states, "should be on a par with the senior teachers in pay and status." So he should be put on the same scale of pay as that of the senior teachers of the school and should have the privilege of enjoying the vacations like the teachers. Unfortunately, the educational authorities in India are still totally ignorant of the duties and responsibilities of the school librarian whose duty, they think, is only to arrange books in the required order on the shelves besides checking out and checking in of books being borrowed and returned by the students. They are, therefore, treated as clerks and in some schools they are made to work in the school office during vacations! And in some of the schools where they are treated as members of the faculty, they are not given the same emoluments as that of the teachers. Professional assistants too are to be on a par with the members of the teaching faculty in pay and status. The authorities concerned with school education today, would do well to mull what Radhakrishnan said in his essay 'The Library Movement,' regarding librarians in general: "If the general level is to be raised, the librarians themselves will have to respect their position as one not inferior to any other and the public should recognize them as such, by securing for them adequate financial emoluments."

No doubt, to some extent emoluments are a factor that determines the status and the respect a professional would command and be recognized by the society. Nevertheless, as is the case in any profession, the school librarian also would command the respect of his colleagues and students as well as the society in general, if he or she excels in the profession. As Tagore rightly points out in his essay on 'What Makes a Library Big', "the worth of a librarian I would gauge by his power of attracting and looking after such (special) circles (of readers), of acting as the intermediary for an intimacy of relationship between reader and library. That is to say, on him is cast the burden not only of the books, but of their readers as well. And in the maintaining of both is the test of the efficiency of the proper discharge of his trust." Although Tagore has written this in relation to public librarians, this is equally if not more true of school librarians also. As I said earlier, the school librarian should know his clientele individually as much as he knows the resources of the library. In fact, this is applicable not to the librarian alone but to the entire library staff, not excluding the attendants, of the school library.

Basically a specialist in library and information science, the school librarian is, in the context of our country today, an educator, a facilitator, a manager, an appraiser and above all, a social worker. And now with the advent of the computer he has become a disseminator of information too. In this digital age, therefore, a redefinition of the role of school librarian is called for. Soon he is to become an information navigator helping researchers to retrieve information from the resources of the Internet and other digitised collections. As discussed already, he will be not only a disseminator of information but a coach as well. And as a coach he will be guiding the researcher who does not know where and how he can find the information that he requires and instructing those who do not know how to use the computer and what are the various search engines that give information on different subjects.

Let alone the fact that few schools in our country have proper libraries, there is hardly any school that has a library big enough, which calls for more than one professional librarian. In other words, the strength of the library staff is determined by three factors: (1) the total enrolment of the school; (2) the educational programmes of the school library; and (3) the vastness and annual additions to the collection. But howsoever small a school is, the need for a professional librarian is as much as it is for a mathematics teacher or far greater than that for a crafts instructor. It is difficult to understand the mindset of the educational authorities who insist on schools having a physical training instructor but do not find the need to have a professional librarian.

Anyway, in most schools that have well-equipped libraries and a huge collection, there would only be one full-time professional librarian and an attendant. In a few of these schools, the professional librarian is burdened with clerical work like ordering books and periodicals, sending reminders and other correspondence also. In some schools, however, the clerical work is done by one of the administrative staff of the school office and so it may be said the school library has one professional librarian, an attendant and a part-time or what may called 'a half' clerical staff. If, however, there is a full-time clerk in the library, the librarian would be able to devote his time entirely to guiding research as well as instilling the reading habit in the children and helping them select recreational reading material aiming at improving their reading taste. It will also give him enough time to quickly skim the new additions before they are released so that he has an idea of all the books in the library; and he will get sufficient time for shelf study.

In Western countries, pupil volunteers of middle and high school classes do the routine work like replacing the books returned by the readers, during recesses. This would not be difficult for them because as we saw in chapter 2, 'Aims of the School Library,' by the time they come to the upper primary section, they would have mastered alphabetisation and got an idea of the classification system. They would have, therefore, no difficulty in putting back the books in their proper places on the shelves. It is also possible to take the help of student volunteers who have good handwriting for accessioning books, which I had successfully tried out. The incentive was the privilege of borrowing first whatever new books they are interested in. Now, with the introduction of computers in the library, handwriting is not a problem. Any volunteer who is a computer literate can be instructed what and how to enter in each field and entrusted with the task of accessioning books.

That many private schools in India even if they have good libraries do not have the necessary funds to appoint professional librarians, is a fact that cannot be overlooked. At the same time it has to be ensured that those schools which have fairly good libraries should have librarians who have the necessary technical qualifications to manage libraries. But with the shoe-string budgets of these schools, it may be difficult for them to appoint full-time professional librarians. This difficulty can be obviated if teacher-librarians are put in charge of those libraries.

A teacher who has undergone training in library techniques and takes care of the school library in addition to his or her teaching work is called a teacher-librarian. The schools concerned can depute a teacher who, according to the Headmaster, is interested in books and reading, to undergo a shortened three-month certificate course in librarianship during the summer vacation so that he gets a practical training in the management of a library. During the three months, he may be given a stipend in addition to his regular salary. If the summer vacation is less than three months the rest of the days may be treated as leave or special leave with full pay. This professional category had come into being in the western countries because several private schools are unable to afford a full-time professional librarian due to paucity of funds. Even many aided schools may follow this example and in fact, even the government schools in our country can adopt this as a temporary measure until they are able to find professional librarians.

During the training course the teacher will be imparted practical training in classification and cataloguing as well as library management, which will give him an idea of the essential registers that have to be maintained in the library. The course should also concentrate on familiarising him with children's literature in the regional language and English, with children's reading interests and methods in the library and lastly with resource books and reference service. In case the state concerned has adopted the three-language formula, the syllabus should include children's literature in Hindi also.

After he takes over as teacher-librarian, he may have to keep the library open for an hour before the school commences and an hour or an hour and a half after the school time in the evening every day. In order to compensate for it, his teaching load must be a few periods less than the minimum number of teaching periods stipulated in the Educational Rules of the State concerned for a teacher. In spite of that, he will have to spend more time in the library to carry out the technical and clerical work connected with the library and so he has to be given a suitable compensatory allowance also commensurate with the additional work he does.

Thanks to the electronic revolution leading to unprecedented developments taking place in the field of educational technology, the school librarians have come to realise the need to adjust themselves to the new situation. In other words, there is, if not there has to be, think on the part of the school librarian regarding his role or function. He is, today, not what he had been all these years. He is not just an administrator taking care of the resources or a technical expert keeping the resources properly organised so that the library works like a well-oiled machine; nor is he a mere educator, teaching the children the use of the library and books, nor a facilitator helping the students and teachers to retrieve the information they are looking for. He is all these. But even when the children learn to retrieve information from the internet by clicking a mouse or tapping the touchpad with a finger, the school librarian does not become redundant! He has to select e-books and e-journals for the library, make sure subscriptions to these are paid on time, disseminate information and help the children who carry on research as well as monitor and guide their general reading.

Hence, whether it is professional librarian or teacher-librarian, when the library is fully computerised and e-books replace printed documents, there will be a drastic change in the role of the librarian. The school librarian will be more an information disseminator than a library science specialist or an educator. When printed books disappear altogether from library shelves yielding place to e-books and compact racks taking the place of book shelves, he may not have to think of classifying and cataloguing; nor would he have to spend time checking the format of newly acquired books. The most difficult problem for the school librarian would be book selection and preventing the children from browsing the internet aimlessly and visiting undesirable web sites that carry pornographic materials. That problem can be obviated if all computers in school libraries have web filters that is, software that shuts out undesirable sites and precludes the children accessing them. This is, thus, a period of transition for the library, library services and the profession of librarianship.

7
Technical Matters

The term library, whether it is e-library or the traditional library of today, presupposes books. When someone says, "I am going to the library" it is understood that he is going to the institution where select books are housed with the intention of reading a book or magazine or borrowing a book or more for reading at home. Even if you say virtual library, you are speaking of books that can be accessed for reading or reference via the computer or any other electronic means. There are non-book libraries too like those with collections of manuscripts, CDs, DVDs and films but they are referred to prefixing the kind of material that is housed in that institution as for example, 'manuscripts' library, 'film' library and so on.

Hence the most important technical matter that a librarian is concerned with is selection of books for the library. In other words, this is the most important function of the librarian, particularly the school librarian, from technical as well as academic point of view. It is, *ipso facto*, the most difficult task too that has to be faced with utmost sense of responsibility – responsibility to the clientele, which in the final analysis is the community that the library serves. When it is said books for the library must be selected with a sense of responsibility, it means the books have to be selected taking into cognisance the curricular and co-curricular demands of the school as well as the intellectual and educational level of the children and the requirements of the teaching and non-teaching staff. The importance of book selection does not vanish with the replacement of printed books by e-books. The qualities necessary for a school librarian that we discussed in the previous chapter come into play in the selection of books. To put it differently, the selection of books that a librarian makes is the touchstone of the qualities of a good and committed school librarian.

It has been repeated *ad nauseum* by many librarians and educationalists that a library is not just a collection of books. A huge collection of books housed in an architecturally attractive building does not make a good library. It is the use to which the select collection of books is put that makes a book collection, a good library. And this is what the school librarian should bear in mind when selecting books because it is the selection and not the collection that matters. A small collection of books selected intelligently with the interest of the clientele in mind is better than a large collection only to make use of the annual budget or to boast that the school has a library bigger than that of any other school in the town.

The biography of Simon Bolivar, 'Simon Bolivar: Liberator of South America' by Scott S. Smith, a book of nearly 500 pages in small print for example, may not be of any use in a school library in our country. No doubt, the biography of a man like him who fought the Spanish imperialists and liberated the South American countries Bolivia, Venezuela, Columbia, Ecuador, Panama and Peru is indubitably inspiring but a bulky tome like the one I mentioned above, no school child in India will read or need to read. First of all not many in India had heard of Simon Bolivar; nor is the topic included in the history syllabus of any of the Secondary School Boards of Examination in India. On the other hand, the school library is justified in buying a small book of his biography, for that will be read by the children and as stated above, the story of his life is inspiring. That is what a school librarian should think of when he suggests a book for the library – the content should be interesting and useful and the language good and comprehensible to the age group for which it is intended. Broadly speaking, these are the criteria for selecting books for the school library.

Unlike a public librarian who has to take into consideration the interests and demands of a very large clientele, the school librarian is concerned with only a comparatively very small circle of readers whose requirements and interests too are quite limited. Besides, the school library has a clear-cut purpose. However, the one difficulty for the school librarian is to make sure that his selection of books provides a bridge to the college as there would be many gifted children who may be looking for more information than the textbook gives and/or who intend to prosecute their studies. In other words, he has to select a few books in all disciplines including literature that are of a slightly higher standard for schools. These books may not be in great demand like the other books that are of the right standard for school children but it should not be considered a waste. The teacher concerned can bring them to the notice of the students so that, as stated above, gifted children will refer to those books. The librarian would, therefore, do well to seek the help of the teachers in selecting these books.

Before accessioning a book, the school librarian must first examine the book on its own merit – both its content and form, which includes the language and other physical features like the print, illustrations and binding, not forgetting the price of the book and the annual budget of the library. If all these factors are satisfactory, he must look at the book in relation to the curriculum and also to its suitability to the age-group. In some cases, the format and the price may be overlooked if all other factors are satisfactory.

The very term 'book selection' implies a kind of censorship. It cannot be denied that it is a form a censorship. The librarian has to reject books containing pornographic material or/and any passage that might wound the ethnic, racial, religious, class or caste sensibilities of any individual or group of children. Similarly, special care must be taken to avoid books with treasonable material and those that incite children to terrorism or glorify terrorists and violence. Needless to say, books proscribed by the government must be avoided and if the ban has been imposed after the book is purchased, it should be taken away from circulation and kept under lock and key. It should not be destroyed or discarded. There is always a possibility of the ban being revoked later when the book can be put back on the shelves.

The first thing the librarian does on receipt of a book is to accession it, after making sure that the copy received is not defective. It is possible that a few pages could be missing or a form kept upside down when binding while in certain cases, the print on some pages may not be very clear. If any such defect is found, the book must be returned to the publisher or vendor as the case may be asking them to supply a good copy of the book. That too should be checked on receipt and if there is no defect, the book may be accessioned. This register called the accession register is the most important register that every library has to maintain, in which particulars of each book have to be recorded and those may be arranged in columns. They are the accession number, date of receipt, author, title, publisher and year of publication, vendor, classification number, and remarks. The last column, 'remarks,' is meant to note down the date of withdrawal and the reason for it. If the book was lost by a reader and paid for, that information should be noted in this column. However, instead of paying the cost of the book, the reader who lost it may replace it by a new copy. In that case, the new copy could be given the accession number of the old copy and the information noted in the remarks column.

Periodic withdrawal or weeding out of books is as necessary as selecting or purchasing books for the library. And this too must be done with a high sense of responsibility. It is, of course, easy to decide in the case of books that are badly damaged or have become out of date. A book that has not been in demand for more than a year too may be withdrawn without much hesitation. Yet the librarian should consider if there is a possibility of the book being asked for in future. This is quite possible in the case of fiction as well as books on political topics, popular science and travels. Books withdrawn from circulation, except those that are badly damaged and unreadable should not be disposed of immediately but should be kept separately in a closed shelf or shelves for at least a year. If there has been no demand for those books during that period, they may be discarded for good. When a book is withdrawn, all cards pertaining to it in the catalogue should also be withdrawn. A wise librarian would keep the main entry card of the withdrawn book in a separate file as a permanent record of the books withdrawn noting on each the reason for withdrawing it. Before ordering a book, it must be checked with this register to see if an earlier copy of it had been purchased and withdrawn and what the reason was for withdrawing it. If it is found that the book had not been popular, it is better to give a second thought before taking a final decision on purchasing a new edition of the same book.

It is essential to maintain a register of books withdrawn, noting down against each item the reason for weeding it out. At the end of the year, this list must be presented to the headmaster and his signature obtained. The headmaster is expected to verify the discarded books physically and countersign in the register, stating "physically verified and found correct." After a year, before discarding them for good, if faculty members are interested in any of those books, they may be given those books gratis or at a nominal price. The rest too can be sold at a nominal price to the public, about which a notice may be put up in front of the school and a few copies of it sent to the office of the local panchayat or municipality as the case may be, requesting them to give publicity to the proposed sale. Whatever remains still may be sold by weight to old paper vendors. The details of the sail must be noted against each book in the register and the proceedings of the sale of the withdrawn books may be dealt with as per government/school rules. In the case of private schools the librarian must persuade the management to add it to the library budget.

The books that are purchased have to be properly classified and catalogued. The librarian should not try to devise his own system of classification. There are several systems of classification devised by experts and in use in various libraries around the world. Several librarians in our country prefer Ranganathan's Colon Classification

System because it is designed with Indian situation in mind and is well-suited to libraries in India. True. It does meet the demands of libraries in India. No other classification system has dealt with indological subjects or subjects specific to India, in such detail. Besides, it is a micro-classification and can classify a book to the maximum depth. Its greatest drawback, however, is that it is highly complicated and is very difficult for children and even for adults who have not undergone a course in library science to understand. Consequently, the juvenile readers would find it extremely difficult to locate a book on the shelf even if they get the call number. Similarly, it would be difficult for the library assistants and student volunteers who are not trained in library techniques to replace the books in the shelves. In any library that has classified books according to the Colon System, it has been found, the books are invariably misplaced.

Of all the systems of classification, in my opinion, the most suited for school libraries is the Dewey Decimal System. The greatest advantage with the Decimal System is that it is easy to operate, unlike the Colon system. Apart from the multi-volume *Complete Decimal Classification and Relative Index*, which is an exhaustive work that could be used in large libraries, there are two other smaller editions that smaller libraries can use. An 'Abridged' version designed for small libraries is advised for secondary/Upper Primary school/primary school libraries. There is another still more abridged 'Outline' version that can be used for libraries of kindergarten schools. The Outline version can be also used as a guide for the librarian when he instructs children in classification.

The Dewey System is based on subject and decimal division and hence is called the Decimal Classification. Being based on decimal system, knowledge is divided into ten subjects and the main subject headings are numbered in hundreds. As such the call number is not spoken as integers but as decimals. For example the call number 364.13 for "Crimes and Offences against the State" is not said as "three hundred and sixty four (point) one / three" but as "three / six / four (point) one / three." The books are first classified subject-wise and so all books on a particular subject will bear the same class number.

How then are these books individualised? The number that individualises the book is called the book number. Let us take for example, books of fiction. In a library there may be hundreds of books of English fiction and all of them would be bearing the class number 823. So when classifying a book like *Midnight's Children* by Salman Rushdie, after allotting the class number 823 (English fiction) it may be separated from other books of English fiction by adding 'RUS,' the first three letters of the author's surname as book number. Thus, novels by John Steinbeck, Anita Nair and Charles Dickens will have 'STE,' 'NAI' and 'DIC' respectively as book numbers. In the case of authors' names like Ulloor S. Parameswara Iyer, some librarians may give the number 'PAR' while some others may give 'IYE'. Similarly in the case of Anita Nair, the book number may be 'ANI' or 'NAI.' If there are books in the library by Charles Dickens as well as Monica Dickens, you may use the first thee letters in the case of the more famous author and the first four letters on the books of the lesser known novelist. Or, you may use chronological criterion – three letters may be used for the earlier writer and four for the later writer.

Whatever is the book number decided upon must be adhered to and used consistently. The book numbers individualise the books that fall under the same class and the same method is used to individualise books in the case of books in all other classes also. If there are many books on butterflies all those books will bear the number 595.7 and a reader who wants a book on butterflies written by a particular author as for example *Butterflies of the Andamans* by Prashanth Mohanraj and K. Veenakumari, will have to look through all those books that are in the shelf or all the cards bearing that number, in the catalogue. So these are individualised by using the surname of the first author and the call number of the book by Prashanth Mohanraj will be 595.7 / MOH.

The main classes of the Dewey Decimal System are,

000 General Works

100 Philosophy

200 Religion

300 Sociology

400 Philology

500 Natural Science

600 Useful Arts

700 Fine Arts

800 Literature

900 History

Each of these classes is divided into ten secondary divisions that fall within the main class, as for example, science is divided into different subjects as follows.

500 Natural Sciences & Mathematics

510 Mathematics

520 Astronomy & allied sciences

530 Physics

540 Chemistry & allied sciences

550 Earth sciences

560 Palaeontology, Pale zoology

570 Life Sciences

580 Botanical sciences

590 Zoological sciences

Each of these is again sub-divided into ten sections like, 590 – Zoological Sciences; 595 – Worms and Insects; 595.7 – Insects; 595.78 – Lepidoptera and 595.789 Butterflies. These are again broken down into smaller sections. But in a school library the classification need not go beyond two or at the most three decimal places in certain cases like the example shown above. Children usually run after butterflies to catch them and as such the 'butterfly' is a topic that most children are interested in. It is not necessary to go deeper than this in a school library. In school libraries, the stage at which it is to be stopped is ideally two decimal places except in cases like the example dealt with above.

Many librarians doubt the suitability of Dewey Decimal system to Indian schools because it is very much American-centred. This is a genuine doubt. Melvil Dewey, the librarian who designed this system was an American and obviously, he had only American libraries in mind when he worked on it. Perhaps he did not expect libraries outside America to adopt this system. Today, however, many countries are using it because this is not very rigid and can be adapted to meet the demands of libraries in any country, whether it is India, Japan, England or Cuba. Certain classes like 'Religion,' 'Language,' 'Literature,' and to some extent even 'History' are designed to meet the requirements of American libraries and to some extent European libraries too but certainly not Indian libraries.

Nevertheless, libraries in India would have no problem in using this system. In the introduction to the

Scheme, suggestions are given as to how the system could be modified and adapted to suit the requirements of any country. So there would be no difficulty in adopting this system for school libraries in any State in our country. But the librarian must take care to ensure that the adaptations should not complicate the classification system and mar the basic characteristic of the Decimal System, which is simplicity. It is this characteristic that makes the Decimal System the most suited one for school libraries (and even college and public libraries.) A problem in modifying an existing system is that it may lead to confusion and any alteration that is made to the original system must, therefore, be noted in the Index and at the relevant place in the schedule.

So the system does provide for such adaptations and it is up to the librarian concerned to do this. For example, under the class 200 'Religion' comparative religion and all non-Christian religions are grouped together in the sub-division 290 and 294 is allotted to 'Religions of Indic Origin' and in India there are several religions and religious sects other than Islam and Christianity. However, if this system is being adopted in a school library in India, the sub-division 294 may be expanded as follows:

294.1 Hinduism

294.2 Buddhism

294.3 Jainism

294.4 Sikhism

Hinduism may further be divided as follows:

294.12 Vedic

294.13 Post Vedic

294.14 Saivism

294.15 Vaishnavism

294.16 Arya Samaj

294.17 Brahma Samaj

294.18 Smartha

Similarly Buddhism can be sub-divided as for example 294.21 Mahayana and 294.22 Hinayana. Any such expansions or modifications can be made in the same way.

There are still other religions as for example Shintoism and Taoism. These may be accommodated by prefixing the letters of the alphabet to 299 (Other Religions) as for example, A299 for Shintoism and B299 for Taoism. Similarly, the different sects of religions like Islam may also be subdivided by prefixing the distinguishing letter to 297 (Islam) like A297 for Ahmadiyas, B294 for Bahai, C294 for Shias and C294 for Sunnis and so on. Please note these are arranged not in the order of importance or the number of people espousing each religion or sect but in the alphabetical order of the names of these religions or religious sects.

The Dewey System generally divides knowledge by subjects. There is, however, one exception and that is 'Literature.' Subjects are irrelevant in the case of 'Literature.' No one asks for or searches a literary work by subjects. On the other hand, they look for a literary work by language and by form. For example, a reader who wants a book by Moorkoth Kumaran, a Malayalam writer, will go and search in the shelf where Malayalam books are kept and then by form – under 'Fiction' if he wants a novel or short story book written by Moorkoth or under 'Poetry' if he wants Moorkoth's books of poems or under essays, if he wants a book of essays written by Moorkoth. The subjects dealt with in literary essays are irrelevant. That is why literary works are classified first by languages and then according to their forms.

When classifying books for school libraries, the librarian has to think of the children first and then the subject. Sometimes, classifying a book under its subject may result in the children not seeing the book at all. For example, the book 'Stories from the Bible' should strictly be classified under the Class 'Religion.' But children seldom go to the shelf where books on religion are kept. So a wise librarian would go by the spirit of classification and not by the letter. The spirit of classification is the primary purpose of classification which is to ensure the reader finds his book and the book finds its reader. If the school librarian wants this to be achieved, he should classify the book, 'Stories from the Bible' not as 'Religion' but as 'Fiction.' The class number should represent the language of the book also. If it is English or whatever is the language in which the book is written, it has to be shown in the number so that the book goes to the proper shelf. Supposing the book is in Hindi, the letter allotted for 'Hindi' may be prefixed to the decimal number. In the Dewey classification, the number '890' represents 'Other Languages'. So if the distinguishing letter given to 'Hindi' is 'D' the class number of the said book would be D893.

In school libraries, it is desirable to separate children's books from the others and so if the library is using Decimal Classification, the letter 'J' may be *suffixed* to the call number of all children's books, irrespective of the class. So children's books on any topic related to chemistry will bear the class number 540J; or if it is a story book in Hindi for children, the number will be D893J.

Once a book is classified, it has to be catalogued, for it is the catalogue that helps the reader to get easily the book he wants. The catalogue is an important tool in the hands of the librarian also. He may not remember what all books are in the library and so when ordering a book for the library, he can find out from the catalogue if a copy of the book is already in the library and if so, which edition it is. He can then decide if it is necessary to buy another copy of the book. Apart form that, many a time, the reader may approach him asking for books dealing with the topic of his interest. Unless there is a catalogue, the librarian may not be able to help him, for no human being can remember what all topics are discussed in each book that is in the library. If, however, he has a catalogue with *detailed analytical entries*, the librarian can pick up in a few minutes all the books dealing with the topic that the reader is interested in.

There are, today, several types of catalogues: the pre-computer age types are the book catalogue, the sheaf catalogue and the card catalogue. The first two of these are not in use today because they are found to be cumbersome and more importantly because they can never be kept up to date. The one that is still used in libraries in our country today is the card catalogue. This too is on its way out thanks to the advent of the computer. After the computer entered the library, more and more libraries are computerising their catalogues but of this too, there are different types. The Computer Output Microform (COM), the Cathode Ray Tube (CRT) or the Visual Display Terminal (VDT) as well as LAN catalogues like peer-to-peer network catalogue and client-server network catalogue. A brief discussion of various types of computerised catalogue that could be adopted in school libraries is given in my book, *The Multifaceted Librarian.*[**] Suffice it to say that the advantage of computerising the catalogue is that it can be linked to the circulation system and can be programmed to show not only the bibliographical details but also location of the book if the school has class or departmental libraries or/and separate libraries for secondary and upper primary/primary sections. In addition, it will show the media, the date of issue, the date of return in case the book has been checked out as well as the identity of the borrower and the reservation status. And school libraries that can afford to have computers have computerised or they are in the process of computerising their catalogues.

But in our country where computers are too expensive for most schools to afford and computerised catalogues are yet to make its presence felt in school libraries, the best type of catalogue that can be thought of is the card catalogue. But sooner the catalogues are computerised the better. The advantage of a card catalogue over the book and sheaf catalogues is that it can be kept up to date always. The standardised size of the cards is 12.5 cm by 7.5 cm (5" by 3"). The cards should be thin and strong with a smooth surface. In case the entries are being written by hand, the cards should be ruled in teal. The top ruling is to be in red and on the left there should be a vertical line in red, leaving a margin sufficient to write the class number or about 2.25 cm away from the edge of the card and about 1.5 cm to its right another vertical line in red. If the entries are to be typed, it is desirable to have a single ruling at the top for the heading. The main entry is the author entry which should preferably be written or typed in capital letters on the top red line (starting at the first vertical line if written in hand). The title of the book is written below that, starting at the second vertical line. The class number must be written in the left margin on the top red line and the book number usually on the line below the class number, but slightly indented. In most libraries the accession number is written at the bottom left of the card and if there is more than one copy of a book, the accession numbers may be written on the same card one below the other.

Apart from the name of the author and title of the book, in the catalogue of the secondary/higher secondary school library, the card should also show the number of volumes, the edition and the year of publication as well as the publisher and the place of publication. In addition to these, some school librarians think it is desirable to indicate on the card, the number of pages, the number of maps and illustrations in the book. This is advised to make children familiar with such entries as these particulars are usually given on the catalogue cards of college and university libraries. But most school librarians do not feel the need for such details to be given on the card as they think that it might confuse the youngsters, for whom all these are not required. Another objection is that preparing such detailed cards will consume the time of the librarian who is the lone professional hand in most school libraries. Instead of that, they suggest, in order to familiarise children with catalogues that have such detailed entries on the cards, they may be taken to the local public library occasionally, to research when they work on class or school projects.

But that alone is not enough. In some regions there may be schools where linguistic minorities are admitted and apart from books in English, regional language and Hindi, there could be books in their language also in the library. It is, therefore, desirable for the librarians of such schools to be conversant with at least the alphabet of that language also. He should be able to read all that is required for classifying and cataloguing books in that language. In a few cases, by reading the title, the librarian will be able to decide the call number. For example, if he can read the title of a book like the *Ramayana*, he will have no problem in classifying. Of course, poetry and drama too can be identified by their 'form' that would be obvious if he flips the pages of the book. Similarly, he would not find it difficult to decide the classes of at least a few books on various subjects like the history or geography of India, and sciences, if he is able to read the title. Anyway, he can ask the language teacher concerned to check the correctness of his decision. But in the case of some books the help of the language teacher may have to be sought for classifying those books.

Needless to say a card catalogue requires a cabinet to file the cards. There are readymade steel and wooden cabinets and it is for the library concerned to choose between the two, depending on the available funds. The wooden one is more expensive but better. In case wooden cabinets are being purchased, make sure that good and well-seasoned wood is used so that it does not warp later and make it difficult to open and close the drawers. The ready-made cabinets may have four, twelve or sixteen drawers with internal measurements of each drawer being 12.5 by 7.5 cm and equipped with removable rods passing through the holes punched at the bottom edges of the cards. The cabinet has to be kept on a stand, the height of which depends on the clientele that is expected to use the catalogue. The point is the cabinet should be at a height convenient for children to go through the cards on the top row of drawers and hence it should be sufficiently low in primary school libraries and a little higher in secondary school libraries.

The catalogue must enable a reader to locate a book if he or she knows the author, the title or the subject. So irrespective of the form adopted, all books are to be listed at least three times – under the authors; under the titles; and under the subjects – as points of access. In addition to these, in high school and higher secondary schools, analytical entries are imperative as these will be of help to the children who are searching for materials when they research on the projects that they would be working on.

Now arises the technical problem. There is more than one form of catalogue and the librarian has to choose the one that he thinks would be the best suited for the library, considering the age group of the clientele that is likely to use the library. The faculty is not a problem because whatever be the form of catalogue, they would be able to comprehend it and use it. Normally, a child may want to know (1) if the library has the book by a particular author that he is looking for; (2) how many books of the same author are available in the library; (3) how many books on the subject are in the library; (4) if a book, the title of which alone he knows, is in the library; (5) whether there are other books that deal with the topic that he is interested in; and (6) in which shelves are all the books that he wants, kept. In the absence of a catalogue, he may have to look through many books spending, perhaps several days in the library. All that time and the trouble can be saved if there is a catalogue which the reader knows how to use. So it is not enough the school library has a detailed catalogue. Unless the children are taught how to use it, the purpose of the catalogue is defeated.

So it is necessary to have a catalogue in which the entries are arranged in alphabetical sequence of authors' surnames. This is essential, particularly in the school library because most children come to the library looking for books of a certain author. Their parents might have told them about the author or in their literature textbook there would have been a selection from a book of that author and that must have got them interested in that author.

Similarly, another set of cards may be arranged in alphabetical order of titles. This query, asking for books by the titles, is mostly in the genre of fiction. So some librarians prepare title catalogues only for books of fiction.

In the case of non-fiction, a classified catalogue would be most useful because the children seldom ask for non-fiction books by authors or titles but by subjects. A dictionary form of subject catalogue would be rather difficult for the librarian to compile and equally, if not more, difficult for children to consult. The problem is in selecting the word or phrase that defines the contents of the book, apart from which more than one entry using different synonyms of a subject or cross references to the main entry may have to be given. It is better to arrange entries in the same order of the schedules of classification scheme. This will help bring together all entries pertaining to a subject including analytical entries. For example, the book 'My Philosophy,' edited by Whit Burnett would be classified under 100 'Philosophy.' A student who is looking for material on evolution would not naturally look through the cards on philosophy and would not know that there is one chapter on 'Evolution' by J.B.S. Haldane in this volume. But an analytical card giving the information will be among the cards on 'Biology' that will take him to the book 100 / BUR.

An alphabetical index is a necessary accessory of a classified catalogue. This is almost like a dictionary catalogue. The points of access are, of course the authors as well as subject names and their synonyms. The classification numbers on these cards are given on the right side just below the title. The author entry is given on the top red line starting at the first margin on the left, below which is the title entry starting at the second margin. The call number is given below this on the right hand side. The accession number may be noted at the bottom in the margin on the left.

The classified catalogue serves two purposes. Apart from its use as a guide to the readers, it can be used *in lieu* of a shelf register. However, when it is used as shelf register, the analytical entries must be ignored. Strictly speaking, it is desirable to maintain a separate shelf register but it is time consuming and it is waste of time for librarian to do so much of clerical work. The time spent on such work can better be utilised for shelf study and helping children researching on their projects and term papers. In fact, a good school digital should utilise the bulk of his free time familiarising with the books that are in the shelves. He must also set apart enough time to look through the magazines that come to the library so that he can draw the attention of the teachers and students to articles of interest to them. It is equally important to find time to take clippings of articles from journals and newspapers and file them. The school librarian should, therefore, spend the minimum time on technical matters. This does not mean that, if there is more than one professional librarian, the one who is in charge of technical matters should completely keep himself out of the academic work and *vice versa*.

Possibly, classification and cataloguing may not be part of a librarian's duties for long. The virtual library has become a reality in our country and its future is assured as computer literates among school children are on the increase as a result of introduction of computer education even at the elementary school stage. And with the increasing production and popularity of e-books, the traditional libraries with rows and rows of printed books stacked in shelves are bound to yield place to e-libraries or librarian libraries. As pointed out in chapter 5, 'Resources' more and more e-books are being produced day by day as it were. With e-books and computers replacing printed books and shelves, the librarian becomes cyberarian and technical work like classification and cataloguing becomes unnecessary. The name of the author and title and such other particulars like the edition and date of publication are all computerised and there is no need for call numbers to access these. The reader can type out the name of the author or the title of the book – even a key word would do – the book would appear before him on the computer screen. He will be able to download it on his computer and read or refer to whatever he wants to find out. Similarly, if he wants to know what all books are available on a particular subject as for example 'Big Bang,' he may type out that and he will see the details of books on that subject.

However, the library and the librarian would not be superfluous. Libraries will exist and so the librarian. The library would purchase the e-books and store them. They will be available only to the members of the library just as how a research scholar is able to access on his computer some of the journals by virtue of his membership of the library today. The librarian of today may then be called a 'cyberarian' and would be more an information disseminator than anything else. He will be free from the chores of classification, cataloguing and all such drudgery. The possibility of pilferage of books will be practically nil and the librarian will not have the problem of security of books. But the dangers of viral attack on the library computers or hacking into them cannot be ruled out. So, instead of the problem of pilferers, the computers in the library could be attacked by viruses and hackers, notwithstanding viral shield and firewall, which may protect to some extent.

Now electronic hand held reading devices, like "kindle" have come into the market and that is bound to boost the production of e-books. The e-book reader is a small electronic device that makes it possible for you to read your book on a display screen of about six inches. The reader can download with the device through a wireless connection any e-book that is available at the store at which the device was purchased. There are over a lakh or a hundred thousand e-books. The e-books are comparatively far less expensive than printed books and the device accommodates over a hundred books at a time, which can be carried in your pocket! It is run on a battery which has long life that lasts for a week and when the battery is down, it can be recharged in about two hours.

The disadvantages are that the owner of this device can download only books that are at the store from which the device was purchased. The dealer is concerned with increasing his sales and profit. Hence most of those books on the list may be of fiction that are currently popular but not necessarily of any literary value or non-fiction books of ephemeral interest. There may be hardly any book in various other disciplines, particularly in the area of your interest. Presumably, these disadvantages may be rectified sooner rather than later.

8

Infrastructure

The objective of schools in independent India has not been to 'manufacture' clerks but, as pointed out in chapter 3, 'Methods in the Library', to produce truly educated boys and girls. The school now aims at imparting all-round education and producing leaders in all fields of activity, as for example in agriculture, industry, and government. That all children in the country are not able to avail of the advantage of school education is a different matter, the fault for which lies not in our educational system but in our socio-economic system. In keeping with the new objective of the school, the state governments in consultation with the National Council of Educational Research and Training (NCERT) have redrafted the syllabi of various subjects that are being taught in the school. The schools in all the states today use textbooks that are brought out by the NCERT or the State Council of Educational Research and Training (SCERT).

This new objective of the school would make it imperative for every school to have a well-equipped library, which, unfortunately, is the most neglected aspect of school education even today. It is a matter for concern that both the central and the state governments have not paid any attention to this crying need. The library today is an integral part of the school but still, even six decades after the British imperialists were forced out of this country, most of the schools in our country are without proper libraries. Fortunately, the governments concerned and the educationalists are beginning to realize the importance and the necessity of good school libraries. In spite of that they have not taken necessary action to provide efficient library service in schools, although it cannot be denied a few states have plans to provide schools with adequate libraries.

First of all, it must be understood that the school library, like the school itself, has two facets – the physical and the spiritual, of which the former impinges upon and at the same time, is determined by the latter. In one word, they interact. The physical facet encompasses the infrastructure like the accommodation, the furniture and other equipment, the resources and the personnel while the curricular, co-curricular and the social programmes constitute the spiritual facet of the school library. In the absence of the infrastructure, the educational and social activities cannot be carried on although it is these that determine the various parameters of the infrastructure. The primary task of the organizer of the school library, therefore, is to study the spiritual aspect of the school library and to plan the former so as to subserve the educational and social programmes of the school aimed at meeting the educational demands and social responsibilities of the school community.

The physical aspect of the infrastructure consists of two parts – the external and the internal. The external part includes the building, the furniture, and other equipments while the internal comprises the resources and the resource persons. In the context of today, when most schools do not have proper accommodations, the organization calls for structural alteration of the existing building or construction of a separate building to house the library, taking into consideration the size of the clientele – the students as well as the teaching and non-teaching staff of the school.

This, therefore, brings to the fore the problem of finance. Whether the existing building is to be altered or a new building is to be constructed, necessary funds have to be made available. The initial expenditure on the school library would fall under two heads: capital and *ad hoc*. The capital outlay is for structural alteration of the existing building or for the construction of a separate building if the existing building cannot be altered for any reason as well as for the purchase of the furniture and other equipment. The *ad hoc* grant is for acquiring a core collection of books, both reference and others. Apart from this, there must be an annual grant for the purchase of books and periodicals and to meet the expenditure on binding books damaged by legitimate wear and tear. The maintenance of the library hall or building will be covered by the outlay on the maintenance of the school building as a whole.

The Government of India had set up, in 1966, a Commission under the Chairmanship of Kothari, which I had referred to more than once in previous chapters for different purposes, to study and make recommendations for revamping the secondary schools in the country. Its recommendation has a bearing on the infrastructure and so a repetition of a part of it is inevitable in this context. Conscious of the difficult financial position of the governments concerned, the Commission recommended the introduction of mobile libraries for serving primary schools in the rural areas. It also mooted the idea of the School Complex, in which the central high school would maintain a circulating library from which books could be sent out to schools in the neighbourhood. This, no doubt, is a good proposition as a temporary measure in the case of a developing country like India as it would save the capital expenditure on the construction of buildings for the library in each school. It would also considerably reduce the strain on the annual budget of each school since books and periodicals for the library are purchased out of the money pooled by a group of schools. But it must be understood, this arrangement will not help the educational programmes of the school library of which we discussed in chapter 3, 'Methods in the Library.' It is desirable that each school has its own well-equipped library on the premises.

This raises the problem of locating the library on the premises, assuming that necessary funds are available. A room or a suite of rooms in any part of the school building may not be suitable for housing the library. In deciding on the location, various factors have to be taken into account. The most important of these are:

1. the total enrolment of the school or/and the strength of each class;
2. the general plan of the school building (or layout of the buildings on the campus if it is a multiple-block school);
3. easy accessibility;
4. the position of various departments, academic and non-academic;
5. natural lighting; and
6. possibility of expansion in the future.

It is, therefore, difficult to put forward a rigid formula for the location, as it depends on the existing building or/

and the land available. However, generally speaking, it can be said that the library must be as much centrally located as the plan of the school building or the campus would permit. But it should be as far away as possible from the playground, and crafts departments like the carpentry, weaving, and such other centres of noisy activity. Several schools in our country are comprehensive schools, meaning schools which have classes one to twelve, some of which having pre-school or kindergarten section too. In such a comprehensive school with the lower primary (classes 1 to 5), upper primary (classes 6 to 8), secondary (classes 9 and 10) and higher secondary (classes 11 and 12) sections, it is desirable to have two libraries – one for the lower primary and upper primary sections and the other for the secondary and higher secondary sections. If the school has kindergarten classes – which comprises nursery, lower and upper kindergartens – also, library of that section may be housed in a separate room attached to it.

This organisation is recommended based on the requirements of the age groups. The tiny tots of the pre-school needs mostly picture books and toys. Although class libraries are desirable in the kindergarten, a separate room is recommended to avoid duplication of books and wasting funds. The standard and the type of books required for the children of the lower and upper primary schools overlap to a great extent. Similarly, the demands of the students of the higher and higher secondary sections would not be different. And needless to say, certain books and other equipment for the pre-school children to some extent may be of interest to those of the lower two classes of the lower primary school. However, if the funds do not allow the luxury of three libraries, at least the pre-school section may have class libraries and the main library can cater to the other four – lower primary, upper primary, secondary and higher secondary – sections. The hall or building housing the main library should be as much equidistant as possible from the different sections of the school.

The Bureau of Indian Standards has laid down standards for the buildings, fittings and furniture of school libraries. This was published in 1976. The Committee that drew up the recommendations consisted of university librarians and professors, architects, engineers, representatives of University Grants Commission, National Archives, Research Institutes and various companies. None of these persons had any practical knowledge about the functioning and problems of the school library, nor do they have any idea of the basic requirements of the school library. The person directly concerned with and who knows the requirements and problems of the school library is the school librarian who is conspicuous by his absence on the Committee. The others who may be aware of the needs of the school library are the headmasters and teachers of schools. They too were not on the Committee. The only thing the Committee knew seems to be that the height of the tables and chairs of the elementary school library should be less than that of the secondary and higher secondary school library! It is heartening that they knew and took note of at least that.

The areas per person both in elementary and secondary schools recommended by the Bureau of Indian Standards are 1 m^2 and 1.5m^2 (approximately, 10.7 sq. ft. and 16.1 sq. ft.) respectively. It is not made clear if this is only for the reader or this includes space for shelving, stacks, alcoves and passages. This again betrays total ignorance of the members of the Committee, about the requirements of the school library. Hence, the recommendations of the Bureau of Indian Standards "relating to Primary Elements in the Design of School

Library Buildings" of May 1977 may be ignored. The Bureau would do well to reconstitute the committee with school and college librarians as well as school teachers along with one or two architects and engineers and redraft the standards for school libraries in India.

In the absence of proper Indian standards we shall fall back upon the standards suggested by the relevant committees in countries like the United Kingdom and the United States of America. The Carnegie Trust Report of 1936 on "Libraries in Secondary Schools" in England recommends 35 to 40 sq. ft. (3.25 to 3.72m^2) for each child. This is inclusive of the space for shelving, stacks, alcoves and aisles. A two-stream or three-stream secondary school in England is expected to have a library of 960 sq. ft. (86.40m^2) and a one-stream school should have a library of not less than 600 sq. ft. (54.00 m^2). These are the specifications suggested by the Ministry of Education in its 'Standards for School Premises.' The 'New Secondary Education' recommends a library of 1200 sq. ft. (108m^2) with an attached storeroom of 90 sq. ft. (8.10m^2). The London County Council Report agrees with the Carnegie Report that the library should have two rooms, one to stack the books and the other to be used as a reading room. In a three-stream school in which two classes with a total of sixty students, will be using the library at the same time shall require a minimum floor space of 1800 sq. ft. (162m^2) and a stack room of 1200 sq. ft. (108 m^2) with shelf space for about 4000 volumes and a reading room of 699 sq. ft. The American Library Association suggests 25 sq. ft. (2.25m^2) per child using the library, including space for shelving, stacks, alcoves and aisles in the case of a school library with two rooms.

The Secondary Education Commission, under the Chairmanship of A. L. Mudaliar, in 1952-'53, envisages the possibility of the library being used by sixty children and five teachers at a time, in a school of 750 pupils with about forty children in each class. So it is assumed, there could be a minimum of seventy-five persons, students and staff, using the library at the same time. If the recommendation of the American Library Association is accepted, the library should have an area of 1875 sq. ft. (168.05m^2) excluding librarian's workroom and storeroom. This recommendation was made prior to the advent of computers. Now that the computers have become inevitable in the school library and if the teaching method is changed to make research an essential part of academic work, the recommendation of the American Library Association is quite inadequate and is not relevant today, as the school library has to find space for computers too. The recommendation of the British Ministry of Education also is unrealistic with computers becoming an inevitable instrument of education today. In the context of today, in a developing country like India the minimum space per reader in the school library, therefore, has to be more than what is recommended by the Carnegie Trust or the American Library Association.

The upper limit suggested by the Carnegie Trust in 1936, that is 3.72m^2 (40 sq. ft.) per reader inclusive of shelving, stacks, alcoves, and passages would be the *minimum* requirement for school libraries with two rooms in our country. That would suffice to have study carrels big enough for each to accommodate a table large enough to keep a table and equipment like the computer central processing unit (CPU), monitor, and keyboard, as well as space for a notebook and any reference book(s) that the student requires. Needless to say, the school should provide internet connection and encourage the students to make use of it for retrieving information.

Hence the library of a comprehensive school with an

enrolment of 750 children should have a minimum area of approximately 202.50m^2 (2250 sq. ft.) which includes librarian's workroom and storage. The length and breadth of the hall depend on the layout of the land and the land space available. This is the minimum requirement and it is desirable to have as large a hall as the land and funds permit so that the need to expand may not arise in the future. If the construction cost has to be kept low the hall may be divided into the reading room, reference room, conference room, work room and storage with glazed partitions instead of brick walls as follows:

The total area of the hall – 202.50 m^2 (2250 sq. ft)

Reading Room – 100.9 m^2

Reference Room – 46.5 m^2

Conference Room – 32.2 m^2

Work Room – 12.0 m^2

Store Room – 10.9 m^2

In the case of separation of libraries of the secondary/higher secondary and the lower/upper primary schools, assuming that the strength of each section is 750, two third of this area or 135m^2 (1500 sq. ft.) would suffice for the libraries. It would be, however, economical and wiser to have one library for the entire school except the pre-school, for this would save the expenditure on the building/hall for the lower/primary school library. The amount that would be needed for that building could be utilised for equipping the library with more computers and augmenting the core collection of books, printed or electronic.

So the organisation and size of the school library are not just a matter of policy but are determined by the total enrolment as well as the strength of each class and the educational programme of the school, not to speak of the quantum of fund available. These recommendations can be implemented without any difficulty in the case of schools for which new buildings are being planned.

In all developed countries like Russia, the UK and the USA, the largest hall in the school building is the one in which the library is housed. The library hall of an elementary school in those countries is usually more than four times the size of a classroom. This, incidentally, shows the importance the educational authorities in those countries attach to school libraries. This should be borne in mind when planning a school building. The location of the library is of paramount importance and as stated above, it should be as centrally located as possible so that it is easily accessible to all sections of the school. Hence, If a single storeyed building is being planned for the school, the library should be located preferably somewhere near the main entrance to the building but not too close to the school office where outsiders may be coming often to make some enquiries or to pay the school fees of the children. Most importantly, the library should be away from the play ground, gymnasium and crafts departments which naturally are likely to be noisy. If, however, the plan is to have a two – or multiple storeyed building for the school, the library must be in the ground floor and as much at the centre of the building as possible.

Many comprehensive schools have more than one block, each of which housing lower primary, upper primary, secondary and higher secondary sections. In addition, some of them have a gymnasium or a hall for physical training with an attached room for storing sports equipment. Almost all such schools have the libraries housed in halls usually in the school buildings themselves. In such cases, there are usually two libraries, one for the lower primary and upper primary units and the other for the rest of the school. In schools like these, it is desirable to construct a separate building for the library to cater to all the units of the school. An important factor to bear in mind when planning the library is its functional efficiency.

The minimum requirements are,

(i) a reading room big enough to seat the pupils of one class and at least an additional five readers;

(ii) a stack room for ;

(iii) a reference room in which apart from the shelves with books like the encyclopaedias, dictionaries, gazetteers and such other reference books, there should be four or five round tables sufficiently large for four readers to sit and take down notes;

(iv) a conference room, which may be used as career counselling room also with one or two book cases to keep materials related to higher educational institutions and careers;

(v) a computer room with at least five computers with internet connections in a school with a maximum of forty children in each section of a class; and

(vi) a workroom for the librarian with space for storage or alternately a separate storeroom.

A large aediculated hall that may be separated into five rooms by glazed partitions with doors, of which one room would serve as reading room, another as stack room the books meant for lending and the other as reference room where reference books could be stacked. Aedicule is an architectural frame around a doorway, niche, or window-aperture consisting of two columns or pilasters over which is an entablature with a pediment that is, inverted V-shaped roofing, like a miniature distyle building. This is recommended so that those who enter the library may keep wet umbrellas on rainy days in case the library building is not connected to the main school building in which all classes are held. This is inevitable in the case of multi-block schools for it is not possible to connect the library to all the blocks.

The reading room would have accommodation for forty-five readers and the reference room, for about twenty readers. The conference room may be provided with a rectangular table or one or two round tables depending on the shape of the room, large enough for ten persons to sit around. Librarian's workroom as well as the storage would occupy the remaining space. These may or may not be partitioned but the walls of this room may be fitted with shelves to keep the new books waiting to be processed and the books meant for binding.

The aedicule leads to the reading room. A glazed cubicle at the entrance in the reading room with a counter should serve both as circulation centre and librarian's work room cum storage. That will enable the librarian to supervise the class in the library while doing his technical work of accessioning, classifying and cataloguing of new arrivals. The entrance to the reference room would be from the reading room.

In order to economise on the building, however, two partitions may be avoided. Instead, shelves carrying reference books may be arranged together on one side of the hall and those with the books for lending separately arranged in another part of the hall. The seating too may be arranged in such a way that table(s) and chairs for those who research are arranged near the reference shelves while the tables and chairs for the others separately near the shelves with books for lending. But the disadvantage is, unless the stack room is separated, the readers in the reading room as well as those who do serious research in the reference section would be disturbed by those who walk about browsing and searching for books in the shelves. Anyway, the conference room and the librarian's workroom have to be inevitably separated by partitions and another two partitions may not add much to the cost of construction. So it is advisable to separate all sections by partitions.

The conference room can be used as career counselling centre also and magazine racks may be fixed on the walls of the reading room. In that case the reading room should have seating accommodation for seating the pupils of the largest class plus another ten readers. A few – four or five – upholstered chairs or lounge chairs may be provided for those who come in to read the periodicals. If the school is subscribing to a large number of magazines, it is desirable to have a separate room for periodicals with not less than ten lounge chairs for sitting and reading newspapers and magazines. In addition, one or two small tables, round or rectangular, may be provided for just two persons to sit and take down notes from the journals. There should also be shelves for back numbers of newspapers and magazines.

But the buildings of most schools that exist today had been planned and constructed at a time when libraries were not considered a necessity in schools and no provision was made for libraries. So some librarians suggest that these schools have to modify the existing building by remodelling two or three contiguous classrooms by removing the walls between them and use the hall thus obtained to house the library, partitioning the hall to separate the stack, reading, reference, conference rooms as well as the librarian's workroom and storage. If classrooms are taken to be altered, there will be shortage of classrooms but if there are rooms that are not used as classrooms, they can be remodelled. Another suggestion is that instead of classrooms, at one end of the building the veranda can be extended to the length required and broadened to the required dimensions and walled up to form a hall. This could be partitioned into as many rooms as required for housing the library. This, however, has one drawback. The library may be at one end of the building and not centrally located as it should be. However, this is better than converting the classrooms.

A third suggestion is to construct a suite of rooms separately not far from the present building with an enclosed corridor to connect the two buildings. Though it may cost a little more, the third suggestion is the most desirable, provided the school has enough land around the building. One advantage in this plan is that the library can be located as much at the centre of the school building, and not far from the entrance of the school office, which usually would be facing the gate of the school compound. The connecting corridor too can be made use of by the school library for placing its bulletin boards for displaying publicity materials like the jackets or flyers of latest additions.

Almost all comprehensive schools will have sufficient land space around the building. So the existing building need not be disturbed in any way and a good aediculated school library complex can be constructed. When a new building is being planned for the school library it need not be just a big room or a hall only.

As the school library is used mostly during daylight hours, natural lighting is of paramount importance and if the building has tiled roof, the various sections of the library should be provided with skylights. In case, the building has reinforced concrete roofing, it is desirable to provide dorm windows to allow sunlight into the library. In addition to these, the windows should be large and glazed to allow as much sunlight as possible. However, thin, transparent curtains may be used to prevent direct sunlight shining into the room. In our country artificial lighting may not be necessary and in case it is decided to install artificial lighting it is preferable to have overhead light. It is better to avoid fixtures on tables in the interest of children's safety. However, if artificial lighting is provided, the ceiling should be of the right colour for reflecting light without glare. All windows should be provided with grilles (gratings) the design of which does not compromise safety of books, cassettes, DVDs and such others that are likely to be pilfered conveniently when the windows are kept open. In a tropical country like ours, where the mercury shoots up in summer, ceiling fans are inevitable in the library. However, if the school can afford to provide air-conditioner in the library, it would be ideal but at present that is tantamount to asking for the moon.

Once the accommodation for housing the library is assured the librarian has to think of the furniture and other equipment for the library. It must be emphasized here that before going ahead with furnishing the library, it is essential to appoint a professional librarian. He is the person who knows what exactly the library needs and not an interior decorator or the personnel connected with administration. There are many things that are inevitable in a school library. The shelves for arranging and displaying books, racks for magazines and newspapers, tables and chairs for the library users, office table and swivel chair for the librarian, book cases, catalogue cards, catalogue card cabinet, vertical file cabinet, shelf list cabinet (optional), lecterns to make it convenient to read newspapers (optional), registers, bulletin boards and so on. In addition, tables for computers and swivel chairs for those using the computers.

There are two types of shelves – wall shelves and

double-faced shelves. Many school librarians had preferred wall shelves earlier but later there was a change of mind among most school librarians. They found that not many wall shelves could be used because of the windows and at the same time wall space which could be made use of for decorating the library with a few paintings and portraits of writers would also be lost. So they now opt for double-faced shelves made of wood or steel. Wooden shelves are more elegant but more expensive and so the school authorities usually go in for steel shelves.

The length and width of the steel shelf are standard that cannot be altered and they are as follows:

Length	90 cm (3 ft)
Width	20. cm (8 in)
Width (for large-sized books)	25-30 cm (10-12 in)
Thickness (if wooden)	2.5cm (1 in)
Distance between two tiers	25 cm (10 in)

The shelves for the library of lower and upper primary school children can be of the same height but those for the library of the secondary and higher secondary school students must be taller. The children naturally grow by the time they enter the secondary school and so the library shelves for the libraries of secondary and higher secondary sections have to be taller.

The heights of library shelves suggested for these sections are given below:

Height –

Lower Primary school	150-180 cm (5-6 ft)
Upper Primary school	150-180 cm (5-6 in)
High/Higher Secondary schools	180-210 cm (6-7 in)

A shelf like this with eight tiers will hold approximately 200 volumes because normally eight volumes take one foot of shelf space. On an average, 30 cm of shelf space will hold eight volumes; at that rate approximately one tier which is 90 cm long will hold 24 volumes and so (24x8) 192 (about 200) volumes can be kept on one shelf of eight tiers. It is desirable that the lowermost tier is about 15 cm (6 ft) above the floor to make it convenient to read the titles on the spines of books as well as to sweep the floor beneath the shelves. Needless to say, shelves without shutters of any kind must be used.

The type of tables and chairs in the library should be not only different from those in the classrooms but attractive and comfortable. These should be arranged in an informal manner unlike as they are in the classrooms. The tables should not be of the same pattern but of different shapes like round tables, square tables and the rectangular ones and tables of the same shape should not be kept together. They should be kept mixed to break the monotony.

The recommended measurements of tables and chairs for the children are as given below:

Tables

For Lower Primary school children – height, 60 cm (2 ft); width, 75 - 90 cm (2 ft 6 in - 3 ft); length, 165 cm (5 ft 6 in); diameter of round tables, 120 cm (4 ft). For seating three children on either side of a rectangular table, its width should be 90 cm (3 ft) and length 195 cm (6 ft 6 in).

For Upper Primary school children – height, 67.5 cm (2 ft 3 in); width, length and diameter of round tables the same as for Lower Primary School children.

For Secondary/Higher Secondary School children – height, 75 cm (2 ft 6 in).

Chairs

For Lower Primary School children – height, 35 - 40 cm (1 ft 2 in - 1 ft 4 in).

For Upper Primary School children – height, 42.5 cm (1 ft 5 in).

For Secondary/Higher Secondary School children – height, 75 cm (2 ft 6 in); width, length and diameter of round tables the same as for Upper Primary School children.

N.B.: The measurements of tables and chairs should not be blindly accepted. The dimensions of the rooms of the library have to be taken into consideration in deciding the measurements of the tables.

The catalogue card cabinet is of standard measurements. There are two kinds of magazine racks – one that can be fixed on the wall and the other that can be placed on the floor. The former is preferable because that will help save floor space. Ready made steel racks of any one of these types are available in the market. If there is a separate room for periodicals, lecterns must be used for keeping newspapers as it would be convenient for children to read them and they will not separate the pages of the newspaper.

In the not too distant future, the collection of resources would be digital materials like DVDs, CD-ROMs and computer data bases. Similarly, book cases and racks, catalogue cabinets and typewriters will yield place to compact racks, computers and e-readers and hopefully school libraries will have printers, scanners and Xerox machines also. These changes will necessitate changes in the measurements and types of furniture like desks and chairs too.

9
Children's Literature

What is it that constitutes children's literature or juvenile literature? The word 'children' denotes boys and girls. However, as it is understood today, when referring to children's literature, the term 'children' denotes literature meant for those boys and girls between five and fifteen. However, when we say children's literature we mean children between three and fifteen because picture books meant for pre-school children fall under the category of children's literature. In terms of students, it includes those in classes starting from the kindergarten to the secondary school. Incidentally, in a study made of the reading interests of children, I have found that generally girls attain mental maturity by the time they are eleven and take to reading adult fiction while boys do about two years later.

What are children's books? This genre of literature includes books written by children and books written for children. It may also denote books written for adults that have been, over time, claimed by children as theirs. The last category, in other words, are books of which the targeted readers were adults but which in due course, interested children and became their favourites as for example, *Grimms Fairy Tales* and *Gulliver's Travels*. Of course, they are suitable for children too and are now generally accepted as part of children's literature.

There are only very few books written *by* children and that too in some of the languages of the world, including some modern Indian languages. It is the other two categories that are usually thought of when referring to children's literature and in earlier days this comprised primarily, the genre of picture books, poetry – mainly rhymes – and fiction. Today, however, there are many factual books of various branches of science, history, biography, archaeology, space travel and all other subjects, not excluding religion and philosophy, written for different age groups of children. And children read them with as much interest and as avidly as they read books of fiction. In fact, some children are interested more in informational books like these than in books of imaginative literature like stories, plays and poems.

The books written by children are known by the term 'juvenilia,' a word borrowed from Latin, which denotes literary or art works produced by an author during his or her pre-adolescent period. There are not many literary works that fall in the category of jevenilia. As far as is known, this term was used for the first time in English by George Withers for a collection of his poems in the 17th century. Apart form that, well-known poets like Alfred Lord Tennyson and John Dryden have brought out collections of poems written by them when they were young and they called them by this term.

Probably Daisy Ashford's, *The Young Visiters (sic), or Mister Salteens Plan* written when she was nine years old could be the work of a real child that falls under juvenilia in English literature. However this saw the light of day only in 1919 when she was thirty-eight years old and *A Collection of the Remaining Novels* the next year (1920). She is said to have dictated a story, *The Life of Father McSwiney* when she was only four years of age and this was published in 1983. She had also witten several plays. Her other works are *Love and Marriage: Three Stories* was published in 1965. *The Hangman's Daughter and Other Stories* (1983) and *Where Love Lies Deepest* (1996) were published posthomously. Curiously, she stopped writing during her teens! She died in 1972.

Jane Austen too had written when she was a teenager. Born in 1775, she had begun writing at the age of twelve. She wrote poems, plays and stories without any intention of publishing but prodded by an urge in her for writing. All her juvenilia were written during her teens, between 1787 and 1793. A novel, *Love and friendship* (sic) is a satire written in the form of letters. Her juvenilia also include *The History of England*, which parodied Oliver Goldsmith's *History of England* which was brought out in 1765. This was embellished by thirteen watercolour miniatures by her sister Cassandra.

There is a plethora of the second category of juvenile books – that is, books written for children in English. Practically everyday, children's books in English are pouring out of presses in the UK, the US, Canada, Australia as well as India and maybe in several other countries like China and Russia too. However, it cannot be said that all these are of good standard and will stand the test of time as for example, the works of Grimm brothers, Jules Verne and Louisa M. Alcott and at least some of Enid Blyton.

In English and perhaps in all Indian languages as well as other languages of the world also there are, as mentioned earlier many literary works that were written for adults had, in course of time, turned out to be as popular with juvenile readers as, if not more than, with adult readers. [As far as Malayalam literature is concerned, I know there are many books of fiction of olden days that were and still are favourites of juvenile readers.] Interestingly, today, many such works of English fiction have begun to be treated more as children's literature than as adult fiction. Into this category of juvenile literature fall many classics including works of modern authors.

Some of these are H. G. Well's works like *The Invisible Man*, and *The War of the Worlds*, Daniel Defoe's *Robinson Crusoe*, Jonathan Swift's *Gulliver's Travels* and several other books. Besides these, Charles Dickens' *The Tale of Two Cities*, *Pickwick Papers* and particularly *Oliver Twist* and *David Copperfield* not to speak of Sir Walter Scott's *Ivanhoe*, Somadeva's *Kathasarithsagara* (Sanskrit), *Aesop's Fables* (Greek), *Arabian Nights* (Arabic), *Grimm's Fairy Tales* (German), Miguel De Cervantes' *Don Quixote* (Spanish), almost all works of Alexander Dumas (French), even Henryk Seinkiewicz's *Quo Vadis* (Polish), that were originally written for adults and still remain on adult classics list. These are mentioned as examples only. Apart from these classics, many modern adult books too are being claimed by children. In fact, most books of science fiction of today and olden days may be classified as children's literature. It has been found that science fiction including those of Isaac Asimov is read more by children than by adults.

In Indian languages also, today, many publishers are bringing out children's books although, as pointed out in chapter 5, 'Resources' the format of these books leaves much to be desired. The problem at present is that school libraries are still in a very bad shape and children's sections in public libraries are not developed enough and consequently do not purchase many children's books in Indian languages; nor do parents think it necessary to buy books for their children. Hence these books have only a very limited market. If school libraries are revamped and begin to function as they should and awareness is created among parents to buy books for their children, the market for children's books will improve and publishers will bring out more and more juvenile books. It must be mentioned here that even though juvenile books are scarce in Indian languages, the concept of children's literature was not alien to India. We find children's books in Sanskrit written in as early as the 6th century CE of which we shall discuss presently.

The beginnings of the story form in literature may, perhaps, be traced back to very ancient times. Although there are no documentary or archaeological evidence to support the claim, it may not be wrong to conjecture that the 'story' was born not long after man learnt to speak as articulate speech presupposes language. That was hundreds of thousands of years before man developed alphabet or even cuneiform and hieroglyphic symbols to express his thoughts in writing. The earliest story that is extant today is a Sumerian myth, *The Epic of Gilgamesh*, which was found on twelve clay tablets unearthed by archaeologists from the region presently called Iraq. This work, written in cuneiform on twelve clay tablets is ascribed to the third millennium, between 2750 and 2500 BCE. Incidentally the episode, found on tablet twelve tells the story of Enkidu going down into the netherworld to retrieve some things that Gilgamesh had accidentally dropped there, is said to be a sequel to the Epic of

Gilgamesh and not a part of the original. Other than this, the earliest stories are, for example those we find in the *Eridu Genesis*[a] and the *Vedas*, which are the creation myths of the Sumerian and the Indian people respectively. The biblical myth of creation, *The First Book of Moses called Genesis* is an adaptation of the Sumerian *Eridu Genesis*.

A glimpse into the myths and legends of the indigenous people of India, Australia and America and the ancient nomads of South African deserts – in short, the myths and legends of the primitive people all over the world – gives us an idea of the origin of 'story.' We find not only that 'story' had its origin at a very early stage of man's history but also that it was actually a record of the events of those times. All those myths and legends actually reflect the times and lives of those people. As Malinowski, the distinguished anthropologist, points out the myths and legends record and validate institutions and are a charter of customs, beliefs, rights and institutions of the period. Levi-Strauss, another renowned anthropologist, analyses *The Legends of Osage*, of an indigenous tribe of the North American prairies and states that it reflects the overthrow of the primitive structure resulting from historical events or events thought of as such like migrations, war and alliance. Similarly, the *Mahabharata*, the *Ramayana*, the *Puranas* and the *Bible* are nothing but compilations of the myths and legends of those times. The *Mahabharata*, the earliest epic extant today, for example, is a collection of myths and legends interwoven into the fabric of the main story the Mahabharata War based on a historical fact. At almost the same time, the Greek writers Homer wrote the epics of *Odyssey* and *Iliad*. And now we have the genres of short stories and novels.

As pointed out in chapter 6, 'Resource Persons,' the

school librarian should be conversant with juvenile literature. In a country like India where there are twenty-two languages recognised by the Constitution, it is not possible and of course not necessary for the librarian of a school in a particular state or linguistic region to be familiar with the juvenile literature published in all those languages. But it is imperative that he or she must have a good knowledge of the children's literature produced in the regional language. In the non-Hindi speaking States that have adopted three-language formula in schools, it is essential that the school librarian should have knowledge of children's literature in the regional language, in English, which is usually the second language and to some extent in Hindi, the third language. But the states in which Hindi is the regional language, the school librarians should have knowledge of juvenile literature in Hindi. The librarians of Central Schools, Sainik Schools and Navodayya Vidyalayas as well as of those schools affiliated to the CBSE and ICSE should necessarily have an equally good knowledge of children's literature in English as well as in Hindi.

Books for tiny tots or children of two and a half to four years of age may be divided into two groups. Those are (i) books that are read out to children and (ii) books that children themselves can read. The former is usually for children up to the age of four and in certain cases, five. These are, in other words, books meant for reading aloud to children who are yet to master the alphabet or to learn to read for themselves. Those books will also help instil the reading habit in children.

In States like the Uttar Pradesh and Madhya Pradesh where the first language is Hindi, few schools, if any, teach any other modern Indian language. The schools in those States teach English as second language and

Sanskrit as third language. The school librarians of those states should be conversant with the juvenile literature in English. In those States if there is any school that has opted any of the living languages of India for a third language the librarians of those schools must have at least a general idea of the juvenile literature in that (third) language in addition to the children's literatures in Hindi and English. Tamil Nadu has rejected the three language formula and the schools that are affiliated to the State Board of Secondary Education teach Tamil as first language and English as second language. So the school librarians of the government schools of the State need know the children's literature in Tamil and English only. In future, if Tamil Nadu changes the language policy and opt for Three-Language Formula, the school librarians must be familiar with the juvenile literature of whatever third language is adopted by the school of which he is the librarian.

As Sanskrit is taught in most schools in our country, either as second language or third language a glimpse into the children's literature in Sanskrit is justified. There are only two or three extant works that could be regarded as the genre of children's literature. The most important and popular work written in Sanskrit for children, is the *Panchathanthra*. In the preface to the *Pamchathanthra*, the author narrates the reason for his composing the stories. Emperor Amarasakthi had three sons, all of whom were mentally retarded. The king felt sad for them and did not know what to do with those boys. So he called an assembly of his courtiers and sought their advice. One of the courtiers by name Sumathi stood up and told the king that it was futile to teach the children different disciplines in detail; instead, all these disciplines can be mixed and fed them in a palatable form. He added there is a person who can do that. That man, he said, was Vishnu Sarma who was a pundit in all disciplines and an authority on children's education. He said, he had no doubt that that man would be able to teach the princes all that they were expected to learn. At once, the king sent for Vishnu Sarma and explained to him the problem. Vishnu Sarma agreed to teach the princes and within six months, he imparted statecraft to the princes through fables, a compilation of which is the *Panchathanthra*. The circumstances that led to the origin of this book narrated above as mentioned in its preface prove beyond doubt that it was written for children.

The *Panchathanthra* which is a collection of fables, the characters of which are mostly animals, is generally believed to have been compiled some time before the 6th century AD although some scholars ascribe it to the 4th century AD. Besides this, there are also other works of children's literature in Sanskrit. Another book that is presumably written for children is the *Sreeramodantha*. This is an abridgement of Valmiki's *Ramayana* for children, which was written in simple Sanskrit by an anonymous scholar of Kerala but when it was written is a moot point. In the 1940s (maybe earlier too) it was prescribed as a textbook in high schools in Kerala for those who opted for Sanskrit as second language. The *Hitopadesa* and the *Kathasarithsagara* are two other books that are suitable for children but it is doubtful if the latter was written specifically for children. The former was, as could be understood from its preface was undoubtedly written for children.

Hitopadesa is a collection of fables written in both verse and prose, the author who reveals himself in the last verse, is Narayana who states that he wrote it to bring home to children ethical principles. The word 'hitopadesa' is a combination of two words, 'hita' and 'upadesa.' The word 'hita' means 'beneficial' or 'friendly' and 'upadesa' means 'advice' or 'instruction.' As in the *Panchathanthra*, in this work too most of the characters are animals. The exact date of its composition is not known but obviously it must be after the *Panchathanthra* was written because the author seems to have borrowed many fables from the *Panchathanthra*. He added a few of his own also. Probably, as some scholars surmise, he rewrote those stories from the *Panchathanthra* with the intention of improving the style but if he succeeded in his attempt is disputable. Anyway, since he has stated that he wrote it for children this has to be considered as belonging to that genre.

But not so the *Kathasarithsagara*, which was written for pleasing the consort of king Anantha, who ruled Kashmir in the first half of the 11th century AD. This mainly narrates the story of the adventures of the son of a legendary king with all other stories neatly fitted into it. A voluminous dome as the title ('Ocean of Stories') indicates, it comprises eighteen books with a total of 124 chapters and 21,000 slokas (iambic verses of four lines each) apart from narratives in prose authored by Somadeva of Kashmir. A collection of legends, folk tales and fairy tales, this work, it is surmised, was based on the *Brihatkatha*, which was originally written in Paisachi language of South India. The *Brihatkatha* on which Somadeva is believed to have based this work, maybe either the one popular in Kashmir or the *Brihatkatha* composed by a Nepali poet. Unfortunately, other than the name of the author, nothing more is known about Somadeva. Although not specifically written for children, many of the stories in it would be enjoyed by children. In other words, this could be considered an adult fiction that children could rightly claim as a work meant for them.

In Sanskrit no children's books with modern themes are produced and so the schools that have Sanskrit as second or third language may not have books for general reading. Neither writers nor publishers are interested in bringing out juvenile books in Sanskrit because they do not have the market to justify their publication. The sufferers are children who are forced to opt for Sanskrit as second or third language. It is, therefore, desirable that the Central Board of Secondary Education, National Council for Educational Research and Training or Sahitya Akademi brings out story books with modern themes written in Sanskrit for children. Any of these institutions can commission those who have enough command of Sanskrit language to write books for children. They may be asked to translate into Sanskrit popular children's books from various modern Indian languages.

So the genre of juvenile literature was not alien to India. There were only a few works in Sanskrit like these that are extant today, which can be regarded as belonging to the genre of juvenile literature. We do not know if many more books had been written for children in those days. Anyway, the demise of Sanskrit which was the spoken language of the upper castes in ancient India, caused by the increasing use of various dialects, the language of the people in general, marked the eclipse of the genre of juvenile literature in our country. However, those dialects acquired alphabets of their own and literary works began to be produced in them. Being products of the Bhakthi Movement, those literary works were focussed on religion and versions of literary works like the *Mahabharata*, *Ramayana* and *Bhagavatha* appeared in the people's languages. And production of juvenile literature in these languages began only in the 20th century when there was a growing awareness of the need to create the reading habit in children. However, conscious effort to produce children's books in various Indian languages is a recent development and as incentives to children's writers Sahitya Akademis have instituted awards for literary works for juvenile literature.

It is difficult to say when exactly the genre of juvenile literature was born in English. The earliest publications that have now come to be regarded as children's books are the well-known folklore, *Robin Hood and his Merry Men*, which saw the light of day circa 1450 and the legend of King Arthur (Thomas Malory's *Morte d' Arthur* published in 1485 by Caxton). Of course, these were not written for children because at that time, no one in England even thought of writing for children. The first book produced in the West with children in mind could perhaps be *Orbis Pictus* published in what is now the Czech Republic. Strangely, an informational book, and perhaps the first ever picture book for children, this was brought out in 1658. Obviously, the writers of those days in the West were not aware that stories were what interested children most and not informational material.

Strangely, even fairy tales published in those days in the West, targeted adults and not children as for example, *Tales and Stories of the Past with Morals: Tales of Mother Goose*, which was published in 1683 and is now being published as Perrault's *Fairy Tales*. In the 19th century, in 1812, Jakon and Wilhelm Grimm brought out a collection of stories, titled, *Nursery and Household Tales*. The brothers collected these folk tales as part of their research on German culture. Interestingly, they disapproved of this collection of stories being referred to as children's literature. Nevertheless, even in those days the people considered it so.

Recently, a new genre of literature known as young adults' literature is being promoted in the US. This occupies the space between juvenile fiction and adult fiction. Unfortunately, the publishers who are interested in making maximum profit do not seem to be paying much attention to quality of the content of these books. Most of those works, perhaps written by writers at the behest of syndicates, are light – it may be more accurate to say 'cheap' – romances like Mills and Boon series, occasionally verging on pornography intended to titillate the adolescents. Few, if any, books for young adults are written by well-known writers and naturally the quality suffers. The only redeeming feature is the language which is tolerable in most of those works. Nevertheless, American teenagers enjoy those stories and those books are in great demand, maybe because they depict the American teenager's world and mostly stick to the "boy-girl romance and they lived happily ever after" paradigm. Few, if any, have any literary value whatsoever. Despite the hype given to those works by the publishers concerned, they disappear from the market after the first edition or the second at the most and it will be a wonder if any of these works lasts beyond that. They along with their "authors" fade into oblivion.

It is difficult to draw the line separating children's literature from adults' literature. Those that can be categorised as children's literature without any doubt whatsoever are juvenilia, nursery rhymes and jingles. And so are fairy tales. Folklores, myths and legends, cannot be regarded as belonging to the genre of juvenile literature although children do enjoy those stories. Similarly, adults enjoy Harry Potter series as much as children do but that does not make it adult fiction; it is indubitably children's literature. Actually a children's book that is capable of interesting an adult may be considered a good work of juvenile literature. As we saw already, many books of fiction written for adults which are still being read and enjoyed by adults and considered to be adult fiction have been in course of time, regarded as children's books. And today, those books are even prescribed as detailed texts or as supplementary readers in secondary schools. It is, therefore, difficult to classify certain novels as adult or juvenile fiction. In the case of poems, plays and informational books in any discipline, such doubts may not arise because books meant for children can easily be distinguished in these genres.

Perhaps it was only in the twentieth century that the need to bring out books for children was realised by educationalists, writers and publishers. This might have been the result of the spread of education in general and the introduction of compulsory and free education for children that created an unprecedented demand for children's books. The recognition of the necessity for schools to have good libraries and the addition of children's sections in public libraries boosted the demand that brought into play the law of demand and supply. As a result more and more publishers began to bring out children's books. Unfortunately, in our country, many schools still do not have adequate libraries and many public libraries do not have good children's sections with the result market for children's books is limited and publishers hesitate to bring out books for children, lest they gather dust in their godowns.

What books do the school librarians consider are appropriate for children? Apart from those that they regard as suitable for children, they usually consider those that have won the Sahitya Akademi awards, and recommended by teachers, reviewers and publishers appropriate for children. Books that are found suitable for children by Sahitya Akademi and teachers can safely be purchased but the school librarian has to be wary of selecting books that publishers and reviewers recommend. Publishers are concerned with their sales and profit only; they do not care for the literary value or any other aspect of the book and some reviewers are influenced by the publishers. Besides, what is appropriate for the children of a particular school may not be appropriate for those of another school. The easy answer to the question posed above is that the librarian has to select books that he thinks are likely to improve the reading taste of children and are appropriate for the age group. This implies that books without any literary value and those with incorrect language are to be rejected.

Unfortunately, today we see a degeneration of the genre of juvenile literature in the US where production of children's books has become very much commercialised. The literary or ethical value of children's books has been given the go by in favour of price and profit. Of late Syndicates in the US have started bringing out children's books like the Hardy Boy series and Nancy Drew series. The names Franklin W. Dixon and Carolyn Keene given as authors of the respective series are pseudonyms. The books in the series are actually written by ghost writers appointed and paid by the syndicate, which gives them outlines of stories. These ghost writers may be anyone who can write grammatically correct English and it is not the same person who has written the books in either of these two series. No wonder, these syndicated works lack literary value and these are so to say juvenile versions of adult blockbusters or 'pulp' novels. Commercial productions like these syndicated works may help boost the sales and profit of publishers but will only hamper children's appreciation of good literature. The stories are no doubt, very popular and it is said millions of copies of these books have been sold world-wide.

The characters were conceived by Edward Stratemeyer of the Stratemeyer Syndicate. These books had been, of course, an instant best seller from the day it hit the book stores sometime in the late 1920s. The popularity of these books in these two series is being kept up by connecting the stories with all undesirable features of contemporary American society. The last couple of decades of the 20th century have seen Hardy Boys getting involved with murders, drug peddling, malpractices by the medical profession, smuggling and such social evils that characterise the decadent American society. The publisher's advertisement department in collaboration with some book stores would hype new titles with the help of the media. And folders would be sent to educational institutions, libraries and book sellers to all countries of the world where English formed part of the curriculum of schools and that pushed up the sales.

The books in the genre of juvenile literature are not judged by their contents alone. Howsoever interesting the story in a book of fiction is or informative the matter in a non-fiction book is, in the case of children's books the vocabulary should be apposite to the age group of children. The vocabulary should be limited and within the reach of the age group for which the book is intended. Simple language does not mean vocabulary alone; it implies the syntax also. A few short complex sentences are admissible but long winding compound sentences should be avoided under any circumstance. Simple sentences not exceeding ten words are ideal in books for children of five to eight age group. The general rule as far as juvenile books are conerned is, the lower the targeted age group the simpler the language and the larger the font size.

There are different kinds, different sizes and different styles of fonts. The size and style of font depend on the content that determines the age group that the author has targeted. The targeted age group of the juvenile reader determines the size of the font. However, whatever is the age group for which the book is intended, the font size should be not less than fourteen and under no circumstances should it be less than twelve. And of course, the font must be larger in books meant for tiny tots of kindergarten and children of 5 to 8 age group. It has been observed that children are attracted if some decorative font is used for the first letter of each paragraph or, in the case of rhymes and poems, the first letter of each verse.

Unlike in the case of adult books, the format of a children's book is as important as its content – not that the format of an adult book is absolutely unimportant. In the case of an adult book, for example, any kind of paper or any size of font is acceptable but not so in the case of a children's book. A book like *Aesop's Fables* intended for children of five to eight years, the format too has to be appropriate for that age group. Similarly, The book should be attractive both externally and internally. During more than three decades of my experience as school librarian, I had observed that a majority of not only primary school children but high school children as well chose books to read attracted by the appearance of the books. And colourful pictures are also a factor that prompts children of primary schools in choosing books to read..

A book with a brightly coloured cover would find more juvenile readers rather than one with a dull cover. So the book jacket or if it is soft cover, the front cover of the book should be colourful with a picture that captures the imagination of a child. The jacket of *Aesops' Fables* published by Gramercy Books, New York is a good example of a picture that would fascinate any child and to add to its attraction there is a picture on the back side too. The illustrations inside are incredibly attractive. It must be pointed out that attractive covers and illustrations are important not in books of imaginative literature alone; they are equally if not more important in informational books. The artist should therefore read the book that he is going to illustrate and give some thought as to what scene or episode should be depicted on the cover.

Another important factor to be taken into consideration is the margin on either side of the page. Librarians know from experience that children's books are damaged sooner than adults' books and would need binding more often than adults' books. Hence, apart from open binding, there should be wide margins on either side of the pages in books in the genre of juvenile literature. The liberal margins would permit frequent rebinding without the binder's cutting machine trespassing into the printed area of the pages. So in the production of juvenile books, the authors, the artists as well as the publishers and printers are equally important.

Appendix-1
Word Games

GAMES WITH ALPHABET

1. Arrange the words given below in alphabetical order by the first letter:

   Man, Ran, Owl, Zebra, Bat, Van, Dog, Ear, X-ray, Fox, Hop, King, Lock, Gum, Pump, Jug, Queen, Road, Cart, Seven, Two, Ink, Umbrella, Word, Nine, Young

2. Arrange the names given below in alphabetical order by the first two letters:

   Vinod, Joseph, Govindan, Ramanan, Muhammad, Sulochana, Yudhishtiran, Ahmad, Jason, Prasanna, Vaman. Somanathan, Umadevi, Anuradha, Gunasekharan, Xerxes, Yashoda, Prema, Simpson, Manoharan, Krishnan.

3. Arrange the following words in alphabetical order by their first three letters:

   School, Country, Town, Symmetry, Number, Eastern, Knock, Cemetary, Cavalry, Umpire, Ceramics, Window, Under, Nominal, Doors, Quake,

Welfare, Term, Knight, Seven, System, Umbrella, Western, North, Quick, Earth, Quote.

4. Arrange in alphabetical order the following words, taking into account all letters:

   Cotton, Zebra, Pencil, Lamp, Button, Queen, Book, River, Ocean, Wizard Light, Butter, Elephant, Lion, Quill, India, Crow, Stream, Zoo, Jackal, Swan, Sword, Buffalo, Train, Umbrella, Paper, Rattle, Pump, Owl, East, West, Zest, Just, Tent, Under, Olive, Copper, Eel, Queue, Wool, Illness, Tyre, Jump, Race, Injure, Uganda, Rice.

5. Arrange the following alphabetically by their surnames.

   Ramakrishnan Venkatraman, Sarvapalli Radhakrishnan, Jyothi Basu, William Makepiece Shakespeare, Mohandas Karamchand Gandhi, Jawaharlal Nehru, Subhas Chandra Bose, Swami Vivekananda, E. M. Sankaran Nambudiripad.

6. Arrange the following names alphabetically by their surnames/last names: (Children may be instructed how to arrange names beginning with O'Brien and Obeidullah, 'Mc' and 'Mac' and to be consistent whatever way they are arranged. It is better to tell them to arrange them as it is done in the library.)

   Catherine O'Hara, Sean O'Casey, Jacob O'Hara, George McMahon, George Orwell, Muhammad Obeidullah, Joseph MacNamara, Gordon O'Reilley, John O'Brien.

Note: The librarian must give more exercises under each category until the children are thorough with alphabetical order.

Appendix-2
Some Aspects of Reading Interests of School Children

[A paper published by V.M.Mohanraj based on the data obtained as a result of statistical analysis of the reading of the pupils of the Lawrence School, Lovedale since 1959 in the *Herald of Library Science*, V.3, No.1, January 1964, pp. 54-57.]

In their book, *Learning to Read*, the authors state that reading "is a function of the whole organism and is carried on for a definite purpose. For example one may read for pleasure or one may read to carry on his work." The role of school libraries in developing the reading habit in children – be it for pleasure or to carry on the work – cannot be over emphasised. But the school library can carry out this task only in close co-operation with other departments of the school. It is, therefore, imperative for school librarians as well as teachers to have a clear conception of various aspects of reading interests of school children. In this article, I shall touch upon some of the aspects of reading interests of school children.

Reading interest is quite often confused with reading taste, which can be defined as mental perception of quality. In other words, taste is the discriminative faculty or the sense of what is appropriate, harmonious or beautiful in literature, the faculty of perceiving and enjoying what is excellent in literature. It is taste which determines whether a boy or girl can be best satisfied by reading a true romance magazine or a book such as *Gora* (by Rabindranath Tagore). On the other hand, "we may think of interest in the field of reading as determining the area or content within which the person is going to read. For example, the interest determines how much reading is done within the chosen field and the intensity with which the individual works at his reading."

Terman and Lima in their book, *Children's Reading*, deal with children's reading interests at various age-levels. Fundamentally, their observations hold good even today and are a valuable tool for school librarians and teachers who have to guide the reading of boys and girls, particularly of lower age-groups. But these observations were recorded thirty years ago as a result of the authors' study of the reading interests of American children. It cannot be denied that reading interests of children is relative and must be looked at in relation to Space and Time. Times have changed, horizons of human knowledge have widened and consequently children's interests also have undergone some changes. I need hardly say, therefore, that the interests of an Indian child of today differ to a very great extent from those of an American child of 1930. But changes in the world of reality do not produce noticeable impressions on the minds of children of lower age-groups who live in an imaginary world of elves, fairies and mythical characters unfolded by the books to which they are exposed. Consequently, changes in the reading interests of younger children are not as conspicuous as in the case of children of higher age-groups. Therefore, when dealing with modern Indian children of 11-13 and 14-16 age-groups, librarians cannot mechanically draw on the titles mentioned by Terman and Lima. The titles are given by the authors to illustrate certain general characteristics of the reading interests of children. In the light of these characteristics observed by Terman and Lima, current titles have to be thought of to suit the interests of modern children. For example, the age 11 to 13 is a period of interest in both boys and girls in books of adventure and mystery. But writers like John Buchan or R. L. Stevenson do not find favour with a child of the mid-1960s as much as Jules Verne or W. E. Johns. Similarly, social novels of Charles Dickens do not give as much satisfaction today to an Indian boy or girl of 14-16 age-group as those of Rabindranath Tagore, Mulk Raj Anand or even Ernest Hemingway.

Let me draw up a short list of authors found to be very popular with pupils of age-group 11-13 and 14-16 of this school. This list is not drawn up on the basis of a subjective understanding of the reading interests of children but compiled after an objective study of the Issue Registers of this school library of the last four years and only those authors found to have been taken out most frequently are included here (see Table 1 below).

This classification is arbitrary because in the matter of reading interests it is impossible to draw such sharp lines of demarcation between age-groups. To give an example, an author like Edgar Rice Burroughs is found to cut across these lines and enjoy great popularity with boys and girls of all age groups.

A remarkable phenomenon of the reading interests of children is the sudden upsurge of interest in them for reading at the age of eleven (see Table 2 below). These examples are picked up at random and the same trend is found to be revealed in the majority of children. It is not accidental that children start reading extensively at the age of eleven. The reason is that now they

1. have learned to attack new words by using contextual, configurational, phonetic and structural clues;
2. have some familiarity with dictionary;
3. have learned to read silently;
4. have learned to read for a definite purpose;
5. are successful in getting simple facts accurately;
6. have learnt to use ideas gained from reading in new situations; and
7. may read silently at the rate of 150 words per minute and understand thoroughly what they read.

But does this interest which has caught on at the age of eleven continue to have a grip on the child? The average number of books read per pupil in 1961 in this school is given below class-wise. (See Table 3 below)

A cursory glance at these statistics may tempt one to jump to the conclusion that children's reading interests tend to wane after the age of eleven. But an analysis of the type of reading done by the children may present a different picture.

A child begins taking interest in non-fiction books by the time he is eleven years old. It has been observed that as he moves up to classes vii and viii, his interest in this type of books also increases and he plunges deeper and deeper into factual reading. A study reported in

Developmental Reading found that on an average, graduate students read a simple story material at 374 words per minute, a passage from Shakespeare at 283 words per minute, a selection from a college zoology textbook at 265 words per minute and a factual passage from the *World Almanac* at 248 words per minute. The reason for the decrease in the total number of books read by a child in class vii to viii is, therefore, quite obvious. The steep fall in the number of books – fiction as well as non-fiction – read by children of classes ix and upwards is the result of the increasingly heavy academic load. So the gradual fall in the average number of books read per pupil as he moves up from class vi to xi is not due to any waning of interest.

However statistics prove beyond doubt that on the whole the number of fiction books read by children is more than that of non-fiction. (See Table 4 below)

It may be assumed that children read larger number of fiction books because they are able to read story material rapidly than non-fiction material. It may be also because they find greater pleasure in reading story books.

In conclusion, it can be said that most children show a natural interest in reading. As far as these children are concerned, the school librarian and teachers have only to make a concerted effort to set in motion the Second Law of Library Science.

Boys Table 1 : Girls

11-13	14-16	11-13	14-16
E. Blyton	R. Tagore	E. Blyton	R. Tagore
J. Fennimore	Howard Fast	H. D. Boylston	D. du Maurier
E. Rice Burroughs	N. Shute	A. Brazil	Pearl S. Buck
"Sapper"	Mulk Raj Anand	L. M. Alcott	J. Hilton
Douglas V. Duff	L. Charteris	C. Bronte *abr*	Marie Corelli

A. Catherall	Ahmad Abbas	R. Haggard	A. J. Cronin
P. F. Westerman	P. G. Wodehouse	B. Orczy	H. Ainsworth
W. E. Johns	Paul Brickhill	E. Knight	G. Heyer
A. Macvicar	C. S. Forester	J. Spyri	Ahmad Abbas
Henry Verne	A. Conan Doyle	A. Christie	P. G. Wodehouse
Robert Martin	A. Mclean	Mrs. H. Wood	Lloyd C. Duglas
Jules Verne	R. Gordon	Mildred A. Wirt	Howard Fast

Table 2 :

Name	Number of Books Read in a Year Class V (10 years)	Class VI (11 Years)
1 Nair G. K.	12	55
2 Sita B.	38	71
3 Adige M.	12	73
4 Vijaya Lakshmi	86	146

Table 3

Class	Age	Average per pupil
VI	11	49.9
VII	12	43.0
VIII	13	39.9
IX	14	34.1
X	15	22.8
XI	16	19.5

Table 4

Year	Fiction	Non-fiction
1959	5,774	641
1960	12,840	2,049
1961	13,774	2,849
1962	10,729	3,264

N B: Books read in Indian languages and those taken out in connection with assignments, projects, etc., are not included in this.

REFERENCES

1 Carter, H. L. J. and McGinnis, D.J., Learning to Read, McGraw-Hill, New York, 1953.

2 Bond, G.L. and Bond, E., Teaching the Child to Read, McMillan, New York, 1948.

3 Terman, L.M. and Lima, M., Children's Reading, Appleton, 1931.

Appendix-3

Library in Pre-School

It is generally believed that television and later the computer have impinged on the reading time of children, resulting in the waning of their reading habit. While television has found a place of honour in many households, very few homes have even a small collection of books. Fewer still are the homes where children find their elders reading and/or where they have stories read out to them. These little ones are frowned on by public librarians and are kept out of the public library even if it has a children's section. The tiny tots are considered beyond the purview of library service, presumably on the ground that the library is meant to serve only those who have mastered the technique of reading, which is an out-dated concept today when library is not just a place where printed books alone are housed. It is essential that the reading habit in children has to be inculcated at an early age, for which they must be exposed to books and reading situations.

The earliest that most children in our country see and handle books as well as to find adults read and listen to stories being read out is when they go to the pre-school, which is a comprehensive term for nurseries (nursery schools) and kindergartens. Pre-schools are institutions meant for children 'past infancy but younger than school age, mostly between the ages of two and five' and as such, nursery schools admit children of 2 plus and kindergartens cater to those from about 3 plus to 5 plus years of age. This stage of life as Bertrand Russell points out 'is of immeasurable importance both medically and psychologically.' So pre-schools intended for children of this age group are, undeniably, the most important segment of our educational set-up. Ironically, however, these are totally neglected.

Many of those who run these institutions are uneducated and have no concept of education whatsoever; hence they do not think it necessary for pre-schools to have libraries. When it is said that a pre-school should have a library, it should not be taken to mean that these institutions should have a hall or building stacked with books in rows of shelves where a musty silence prevails and children of 2 to 5 years of age are made to read those books. It is insane even to suggest that. The pre-school library is to be equipped with toys, film projectors, television, DVD players, audiobooks and picture books.

Most of the pre-schools are run in ill-ventilated, dingy rooms with one teacher who is generally a person without requisite qualifications, teaching both the lower and upper kindergarten classes. These schools are money-spinners and run as business enterprises. It is, therefore, imperative that all State governments bring in legislations regulating pre-schools and formulate rules like those governing elementary and secondary schools. And they should be monitored by the department of education as is being done in the case of elementary and secondary schools today. As stated in chapter 2, 'Aims of the School Library' it is at the pre-school that most children in our country see and get to know what a 'book' is for the first time in their lives and so the foundation for the reading habit in children should be laid here. However, let alone what may be called a library, few pre-schools which have mushroomed in our country in recent years have toys, electronic equipment like those mentioned above or/and even a small collection of picture books.

A small library is as essential for a pre-school as it is for a lower primary school, for it is the pre-school that has the responsibility to do the spade work for creating library consciousness in children. It must be done at the pre-school. It is understandable that Froebel who was an authority on pre-school education and who even started the first ever kindergarten in the world, had not thought of this as in his days no educationalist thought that a school should have a library. But, as pointed out in chapter 1, 'School Library – Its Rise and Organisation,' by the second decade of the 20th century, library began to be regarded as an integral part of a school and hence it is beyond one's comprehension why Montessori and especially Kothari overlooked this aspect of pre-school education.

The pioneer of pre-school education, E. W. A. Froebel (1782-1852), a German educationalist who stressed the importance of pleasant surroundings, self-activity and physical training for children, suggested that their creative play instincts be channelised to develop co-operation and application and thus prepare them for schools. Froebel who insisted on 'pleasant surroundings,' called the school that he founded in 1817, the first one of its kind in the world, *kindergarten*, the German word, which means 'Children's Garden.' The Montessori system as envisaged by Maria Montessori (1870-1952), the Italian educationalist, another authority on pre-school education, aims at the development of initiative through individual freedom of action, improvement of sense perception and co-ordination of motor activities.

Pre-primary schools, the Kothari Commission (1966) exhorts, should help the child develop good health habits, desirable social attitudes and manners, emotional maturity, a good physique, sufficient muscular combinations and basic motor skills as well as the ability to express his thoughts and feelings. These schools should also encourage aesthetic appreciation, independence and creativity and stimulate intellectual curiosity. This, the Commission feels, could be achieved through play as well as through manual, artistic and handwork activities, physical training and so on. Categorically ruling out a curriculum for pre-primary schools, the Commission recommends learning activities like nature study through contact with the physical and biotic world besides counting and arithmetic.

None of the educationalists think of a library for tiny tots because their concept of a library for children was different from what it is today. As mentioned in chapter 3, 'Methods in the Library,' the age at which children are admitted in pre-schools, nurseries and kindergartens, is when children begin enjoying grandma's tales. So nursery school is the right place to introduce children to books – not that these children are to be taught the alphabet and made to read story books. No, certainly not. But children's natural interest in stories should be exploited to introduce them to books. The teacher can tell them stories holding the book from which the story is taken and as she narrates the story, the illustrations in the book should be shown to them at the appropriate time. And she may even pass the book around for each child to look at the picture for a few minutes, thereby giving the children an opportunity to feel 'book,' for which they would not have had an opportunity at their homes – why, they would not have even seen a book in their homes. These story telling/reading sessions of half an hour, must be a daily routine.

Few pre-primary schools in our country have the most essential educational infrastructure. Seldom do we find even outdoor play apparatuses like swings, slides, sea-saws and monkey ladders in pre-schools in our country. Apart from these all pre-schools must have libraries where picture books for the kids to look through as well as small toys and board games to play with are available. In addition, they should have a television set or discs and a disc player and such other electronic equipment, which would go a long way in arousing children's intellectual curiosity. But the pre-schools in our country, which are basically commercial ventures, cannot be expected to take advantage of the developments in educational technology involving expenditure.

All those playthings mentioned above help open a channel of communication with the children as well as their parents. Care should be taken not to procure any hard toys that might injure the children. Many of the parents and pre-school teachers may not be familiar with sophisticated modern toys that have today inundated the market. So the teacher, after acquainting herself with these playthings may arrange a few meetings of the parents in the school to show them how these playthings work without endangering the children. These playthings are actually a means to introducing the children to books. So the pre-school library should inevitably have attractive audiobooks and picture books which would help children familiarise with and take a liking for books so that they would look upon books as a source of pleasure. This impression would remain in their minds and once they learn to read they would take to recreational reading as fish to water. Occasionally, short educational films of half-an-hour duration may be screened instead of story telling sessions.

In pre-schools, it will be more economic to have one single library for all the three classes because one set of toys and one copy of each book will serve the purpose. But it is desirable to have class libraries – separate libraries for the nursery, lower kindergarten and upper kindergarten. Each of these libraries must be equipped with different types of toys and different books. As the standard of the children in these classes are not very different, if necessary, some of the toys and books can be rotated among the three classes once or twice a year to break the monotony.

These kids would enjoy hands-on work for a change. So instead of telling or reading out stories to them or leaving them to play with toys everyday the teachers concerned may make the children clip pictures from old magazines and paste on a sheet of paper. The children may be asked to paste pictures of any one theme – like birds, tribes, prominent personalities or scenery and so on, on sheets of thick white drawing paper and write under each picture what it is. The teacher may have to guide them in some cases to decide on which sheet a particular picture is to be pasted. Finally the teacher can separate these sheets thematically and get them bound. The old book shops in the town may have back numbers of various magazines like the *National Geographic* that carry many coloured pictures, which an be bought for the purpose. All these sheets with the pictures pasted on them and bound can be made into albums, which would make good additions to the library.

Bibliography

Selected List of Books for Collateral Reading

Adler, M. J. and Doren, Charles Van, How to Read a Book, Simon and Schuster, New York, 1972.

Alabaster, C., Developing an Outstanding Core Collection, American Library Association. Chicago, 2002.

Anderson, P.S., Story Telling with the Flannel Board, T.S.Denison & Company, Minneapolis, 1963.

Benne, M., Principles of Children's Services in Public Libraries, American LibraryAssociation, Chicago, 1991.

Benton Foundation, Buildings, Books and Bytes, W.K.Kellog Foundation, Washington D.C., 2006.

Britton, J., Language and Learning, Penguin, London, 1970.

Brookes, P., Electronic Surveillance Devices, Butterworths, London, 1996.

Butler, D., Babies Need Books, Penguin, New York, 1988.

Butler. D., Saying it Louder, In *School Library Journal*, 35:13, September, 1989.

Calvino, Italo, tr, by Martin McLaughlin, Why Read the Classics, Pantheon, New york, 1999.

Chambers, A., Introducing Books to Children, Heineman Educational Books, London, 1973, p.18.

Cochran,-Smith, M., The Making of a Reader, Ablex, Norwood, 1984.

Craig, D., Preschool Library Service, In *American Libraries*, 4:4, March, 1973.

Datta, B.K., Libraries and Librarianship of Ancient and Mediaeval India, Atma Ram & Sons, 1970.

De Villiers, Peter A. and Jill, G. De Villiers, Early language, Harvard University Press, Cambridge, Mass., 1979.

Divers Hands, The Library Movement, Madras Library Association, Madras,1929.

Durkin, D., Children Who Read Early: Two Longitudinal Studies, Teachers College Press, New York, 1966.

Elizabeth, J.W., Counselling with Parents of Handicapped Children: Guidelines for Improving Communication, Grune and Stratton, New York, 1977.

Elkind, D., Miseducation: Preschoolers at Risk, Knopf, New York, 1987.

Emerson, L.S., Storytelling, The Art and the Purpose. Zondervan Publishing House, Grand Rapids, 1959.

Erkison, E.H., Childhood and Society, Norton, New York, 1964.

Evans, G. E., Developing Library and Information Centre Collections, Libraries Unlimited, Littleton - CO, 1987.

Fargo, L.F., The Library in the School, American Library Association, Chicago, 1947.

Feinberg, S., The Parent/child Workshop. In *School Library Journal* (USA), 31:8, April, 1985.

Fisher, J.J., Toys to Grow With! Infants and Toddlers, Putnam, New York, 1986.

Gour, P. N and P., School Library, Library Publications, Patna, 1982.

Greene, E. and Cullinan, B. E., Educating Librarians to Serve Early Childhood. *In School Library Journal*, 34:11, August, 1988.

Hardendorff, J.B., Storytelling and the Story Hour. In *Library Trends*, July 1963, p.60.

Haines, H. E., Living with Books: The Art of Book Selection, Columbia University Press, New York, 1950.

Harste, J.C., et al., Language, Stories and Literacy Lessons, Heinemann, Portsmouth, N.H., 1984.

Hektoen, F.H. and Rinehart, J.B. eds., Toys to Go: A Guide to the Use of Realia in Libraries, American Library Association, Chicago, 1976.

John, F.H., Serving Visually Handicapped Children, In School Library Journal, 25:4, December 1978, pp. 36-37.

Katz, W.A., Collection Development: The Selection of Material for Libraries, Holt, New York, 1980.

Kothari Commission, Report, 1966.

Leyland, E., Libraries in Schools, Oldbourne, London, 1961.

Lincoln, A.J., Computer Security, In *Library and Archival Security*, 11:1, 1991, pp.157-71.

McCabe, G.B., Kennedy, J.R., eds., Planning the Modern Public Library Building, Libraries Unlimited, West Port, 2005.

McClure, C.R., et al., Planning and Role Setting for Public

Libraries: A Manual of Options and Procedures, American Library Association, 1987.

Mohanraj, V.M., Library Services for Children, Ess Ess Publications, New Delhi, 2004.

Mohanraj, V.M., The Multifaceted Librarian, Ess Ess Publications, New Delhi, 2006.

Morrison, G. S., Education and Development of Infants, Toddlers and Preschoolers, Scott, Foresman, Glenview, Ill., 1988.

Morrison, P. R., Computer Parasites – Software Diseases may Cripple Our Computers, In *The Futurist*, March-April , 1986, pp.36-38.

Mudaliar Commission, Report, Government of India, 1953.

Power, E.L., Work with Children in Public Libraries, ALA, 1943.

PROVIDING School Library Services for the Culturally Disadvantaged, *ALA Bulletin*, February, 1965.

Ralph, R.G., The Library in Education, Phoenix House, London, 1949.

Shedlock, M.L., Art of the Storyteller, Dover, New York, 1951.

Singer, D.G. and Revenson, T.A., A Piaget Primer: How a Child thinks, New America Library, New York, 1978.

Smith-Kanen, S., Socialisation of the Physically Handicapped. In *The Journal of Applied Rehabilitation Counselling* (USA), 7, 1976 (Fall), pp.113-114.

Thapar, Romila, The Penguin History of Early India, Penguin, New Delhi, 2003.

Tooze, R., Storytelling, Prentice-Hall, Englewood cliffs, 1950.

Wells, G., The Meaning Makers: Children Learning Language and Using Language to Learn, Heinmann, Portsmouth, N.H., 1986.

Wheeler, S.H., Children's Libraries, *Wilson Library Bulletin*, December 1964.

White, B.L., Educating the Infant Toddler, Lexington Books, Lexington, Mass., 1988.

White, D., Books before Five, Heinemann, New York, 1986.

Wright, B.A., Changes in Attitudes toward People with Handicaps. In *Rehabilitation Literature*, 34, 1973, pp. 354-357, 368.

Wright, B.A., Physical Disability – A Psychological Approach, Harper and Row, New York, 1960.

Index